Guide to Independent Radio Journalism

Linda Gage

Duckworth

First published in 1990 by
Gerald Duckworth & Co. Ltd.
The Old Piano Factory
43 Gloucester Crescent, London NW1 7DY

©1990 by Linda Gage

ISBN 0 7156 2341 9

British Library Cataloguing in Publication Data
Gage, Linda
  Guide to independent radio journalism.
  1. Great Britain. Radio programmes : News programmes.
  Journalism
  I. Title
  070.1940941

  ISBN 0–7156–2341–9

Photoset in North Wales by
Derek Doyle & Associates, Mold, Clwyd
Printed in Great Britain by
Billing & Son Ltd, Worcester

Contents

3. Responsibilities, Objectivity and Confidentiality

4. Writing for Radio

5. Getting the Story

6. Telling the Story

7. Programme Production

8. The Law and the Courts

9. Libel

10. Contempt of Court

11. Restrictions on Reporting

To Gene Amole, who advised me at the start: 'By all means stay in radio, but whatever you do, don't become a DJ. By the time you're forty, you're sick of saying "here is, that was; here is, that was; here is …" '

Foreword

by the Rt. Hon. Christopher Chataway
Chairman of the Crown Communications Group

Linda Gage has proved herself to be an outstanding trainer of radio journalists. In this book she sets out succinctly and clearly the information and advice that will be needed by any aspiring radio reporter.

As the radio industry expands in Britain more good journalists are going to be required. For almost every radio station an essential ingredient of success will be a fast, lively, honest news service. Already there is a shortage of competent professionals. The standards of reporting and interviewing are distinctly uneven.

So this is a timely and important book. Having started my broadcasting life as an untrained newscaster and television reporter, I can recognise all sorts of mistakes that I might not have made had I been able to read this book. I have no doubt that it will prove invaluable to many radio journalists and that it will help to create a standard of vigorous and respected radio reporting up and down the country.

Acknowledgments

Watching other people get as smitten by radio as I am has always been a pleasure, but working at the National Broadcasting School gave me the opportunity to infect whole groups of people while in return teaching me a great deal. My gratitude goes to everyone there, especially Keith Belcher and Rory McCloud.

This book would not have been written without the encouragement, support and advice of many of my colleagues and friends. Everyone at what was LBC (now London Talkback Radio and LBC Crown FM) and at IRN have consistently made themselves available to me and my incessant questions, but those who endured more than their fair share of my fretting should at least receive a mention.

Lawrie Douglas first suggested I write this book, and he has never faltered in his faith in the project or in me – a specially important support during all those times when my own confidence waned.

Peter Thornton, the Managing Director of LBC/IRN, has always been positive and helpful, and Philip Bacon, the Editor of LBC Crown FM, gave up precious days to wade through the manuscript and make sensible suggestions. Roger Francis, the company's Chief Engineer, managed to explain to me complex technical concepts in words of one syllable, while the difficult job of trying to keep my sense of humour and of proportion usually fell on the shoulders of Robin Malcolm, the Director of Programmes for London Talkback Radio. Vivien Fowle and Sara Jones gave me valuable advice on particular chapters, and Deborah Blake at Duckworth poured an enormous amount of energy and time into it all.

A team of busy lawyers at Stephenson Harwood combed through my original notes on the legal chapters, while Larry Grant never lost his patience trying to correct some of my misconceptions about the law. It is also to his credit that I ate well during all those days of writing.

Introduction

No one is quite sure exactly *why* radio works, but work it does, and when it is used effectively there is nothing to better it. Radio came into its own during the Second World War, when personalities on the 'wireless' got the sort of public respect and devotion accorded to today's film stars, and the tone and delivery of news readers reflected their starched shirts and formal wear. Over the last fifty years engineers have improved the technical aspects to the extent that even the smallest transistor is capable of such good sound quality that the radio is equivalent to a friend in the room, and programme-makers have developed a better understanding of why certain techniques work to keep that friend amusing and informative.

Good and bad points

Radio is fast, simple and, compared with other media, cheap. It is entertaining, informative and intimate. It is also malleable in a way no other medium can be. The Kenny Everett show and the *Hitch-hiker's Guide to the Galaxy* both used radio in an inventive and entertaining way, but arguably neither was as successful when transferred to television. You can take your listener anywhere in radio, but when pictures are introduced the imagination is limited. In the TV version of the *Hitch-hiker's Guide*, the schizophrenic, double-headed Zaphod Beeble-brox was almost impossible to present, but the radio character was credible and funny.

On the other hand, radio is also transient and often only half listened to. People tend to be doing something else while the radio is on. So, while it is intimate, often it is also treated like a member of the family who will not object to a bit of off-handedness now and then. When people get their information from newspapers, that sheet of paper tends to get their undivided attention, which is a luxury radio does not have.

Radio also has severe limits of time and choice. When you read a newspaper, your eye scans the headlines so that you can choose which article to read. If it is a big story, the paper will give it more space. Radio can give major stories more time, but it has to use words and tone of voice to convey importance. A paper can have about 100 column inches on its front page. A three-minute news bulletin is equivalent to about ten inches. Listeners have virtually no choice – they must either listen to everything that is broadcast, or switch off and hear nothing.

The future of radio

Commercial radio is at present experiencing the biggest shake-up since its inception. With deregulation, community stations are likely to proliferate, and *licenses* will be awarded to allow a station to operate, rather than the *franchises* of the past. The body that has been responsible for controlling the industry, the Independent Broadcasting Authority (IBA), is in the process of being phased out and a new body, the Radio Authority, is being introduced in its stead.

There has been controversy about whether quality will suffer under the new regulations and whether there is enough advertising revenue available to support so many new stations. Given the experience of other countries, I do not share the most pessimistic views, but we will have to wait to find out whether the listener will cope, and what adjustments will have to be made for it all to work. The professionalism already available within Independent Local Radio and the enthusiasm for its future seem to suggest a positive rather than a negative outlook.

Throughout this book I have referred to IBA guidance or

regulations, and as the Radio Authority takes over some changes may take place, but the principles of the advice will remain sound. Indeed, the station I have been associated with since 1974 decided to split its service in 1989 – a decision that is being taken by an increasing number of independent local radio stations. [Before 2 October 1989, there was one radio station – LBC. On that day, two new radio stations were launched in its place: London Talkback Radio on the AM frequency and LBC Crown FM on the FM frequency.] London Talkback Radio emphasises the light-hearted side of life with almost continual phone-ins, while LBC Crown FM is a serious news service rivalling BBC Radio Four.

This book is about using commercial radio. It gives practical guidelines on how to convey news and information effectively. But no book can convey the stress involved in getting the story out first, or the frustration of having to edit out interesting bits of an interview in order to make it comply with time constraints. Equally, no book can convey the feeling of magic when it all works.

Glossary

Radio is full of jargon or 'in' words. These are usually defined the first time they appear in the text, but you may need to refer back to this list from time to time.

actuality: Live or recorded sound of an event or speech as it happened.

ad: Advertisement.

ad lib: Unscripted remarks.

air check: A mention of a person, event or product on air.

ALC: Automatic level control. A feature on some portable tape machines that will automatically maintain a standard recording level.

alignment: The process of positioning tape heads or equipment controls for optimum performance.

ambience: The low level background noise which characterises the sound in a room, studio or outside location.

AM: Amplitude Modulation. A method of radio transmission used on the Medium Wave system.

audio: Material transmitted or received as sound rather than the written word.

audio feed: Transmission of sound to other stations or studios.

back-anno or **B/A**: Announcement given at the end of a piece of music, a tape or interview which gives details of what has been heard.

back timing: The time at which an item (music or jingle) needs to be started (before it is needed or transmitted) so that it ends at a precise time (also known as prefading to time).

balance: (a) A mix of different sounds. (b) Desk control for altering the relative volume of left and right stereo channels.

band: (a) A separate section of tape within a spool; one of a number of separate items consecutively on the same tape. (b) Group of frequencies for transmission – wave band.

bass: Low frequency (LF) sound waves.

bed: A theme or signature tune behind an announcer's voice that may be back-timed.

billboard: (a) An American radio/record industry weekly magazine.

(b) An IRN service of programme length material, fed to network stations each hour during weekdays.

booth: A small recording studio, usually designed to accommodate one or two people, for pre-recordings.

breaking story: A story that is happening now.

break-up: An audio fault causing sound to come and go intermittently.

bulk eraser: A machine designed to erase or 'wipe' a tape or cartridge all at once. Use with caution!

cans: Headphones.

capstan: Drive spindle on a tape machine.

cartridge: (a) A fixed duration, endless loop of tape on a spool in a sealed plastic case, available in different lengths, e.g. 40 secs or 100 secs. Nearly always referred to in abbreviated form as **cart**. (b) The head of a turntable arm which contains the stylus.

cassette: Reels of tape for a cassette recorder in a sealed plastic case.

catchline: Also known as **slug**. The word or words at the top of a script which identifies the story.

CD: Compact disc.

Cellnet: A cellular telephone network which uses battery-operated telephones.

centre: (a) An adaptor for tape machines to enable them to take 10.5 inch spools, known as NAB spools. Hence also NAB centre or NAB adaptor. (b) An adaptor for 45 rpm discs with large centre hole.

Ceefax: BBC TV news and information text service receivable on teletext TVs.

circuit: An audio line rented from BT which is either one-way, studio quality (a 'music' or wideband circuit) or lesser quality for cue programme or two-way talkback which is roughly equal to a telephone line (a 'control' or narrowband circuit).

clean feed: Output as it comes from the source or studio, without over-riding commentary or other incoming sources. Abbreviated to C/F.

clip: An extract from a programme or film.

channel: A single source on an audio desk.

Comrex: A device, usually one-way, for enhancing telephone quality reports.

contribution network: A network of audio circuits by which IRN can take in good quality audio material from any ILR station.

copy: Written news or information.

cps: Centimeters per second. The speed at which tape is travelling past the heads, usually 19 cps for speech, and 38 cps for music (see **ips**).

croc-clips: Connectors to feed the output of a tape recorder via a telephone.

cross-fade: Fading out one source while fading in a new one.

crosstalk: Interference caused by breakthrough of signals from one circuit or tape track to another.

cue: (a) Written introduction to a tape or live interview. (b) A signal by hand or by a light for the next item or person to begin.

cue programme: programme or audio usually fed to a person's headphones that introduces or indicates when that person should start broadcasting, e.g. from a studio to an outside broadcast unit.

cut: A short excerpt from a longer piece of taped audio, usually on cart.

dB: Decibel. Unit of intensity of sound. Used to measure 'loudness'.

delay: Transmitting a programme three to ten seconds later than it happens live in order to be able to over-ride libels, profanities, etc. Also known as 'being in prof.'.

desk: An electronic control panel (and the furniture around it) for mixing different sources.

distribution network: A network of audio circuits by which IRN can send out good quality audio material to all the ILR stations.

DJ: Disc jockey, sometimes called a jock.

double-header: Item or programme presented by two people.

drive time: Morning and afternoon commuting times with the highest number of in-car listeners.

drop-out: A momentary break in the audio output of a tape caused by a fault or a bad splice.

dub: A copy from one source to another, i.e. cassette to tape, tape to tape.

dur.: Duration.

edit: To remove unwanted recorded material by splicing the tape.

embargo: A request to hold publication of a fact or event until a specified date and time.

erase: To remove all sound from a tape – on purpose or accidentally! Also known as 'wiping'.

EQ: Equalisation. Using special controls to alter the sound quality, by increasing or decreasing sounds in the high, middle or low frequency sound ranges. Equivalent to the 'bass' and 'treble' controls on a domestic hi-fi.

fader: Slide mechanism on the desk to alter the volume.

Faraday: The BT centre for switching and booking audio circuits.

featurette: see **wrap**.

feed: Supply of audio by circuit or line.

feed-back: Same as 'howl-round'.

fixed spot: An item that regularly features in a programme.

FM: Frequency Modulation. A method of transmission used on VHF radio and some TV sound transmission.

fluff: (a) The accumulation of dust on a stylus. (b) To make a mistake while reading copy.

flutter: Accelerated version of wow.

full track: Recording which uses the full width of the tape.

FX: Sound effects, either intrinsic in the recording, or added from another source.

gram: Record turntable.

half-track: Method of recording which uses only half the width of the tape in one direction and the other half in the other direction, e.g. on cassette, but this is also a feature on some reel-to-reel machines.

hash: Crackling sound interference, like frying bacon.

head out or **H/O**: A tape which is rewound, ready to be played on a tape machine.

heads: (a) Parts of a tape recorder which erase, record and playback. (b) Headlines. One-sentence summaries of the main four or five stories. Also known as 'Highlights'.

HF: (a) High frequency, the treble sounds. (b) The 'Short Wave' broadcasting band.

high level switcher: A switcher on a mixing desk enabling different or short-term external sources to be faded up on the desk, usually plugged through to the desk from MCR.

hiss: Background noise, usually barely discernable. Also known as 'tape hiss'.

howl-round: High-pitched tone created by high-level sounds feeding back through a live microphone.

hum: Low frequency tape interference, usually caused by electrical mains.

ID: Station identification.

ILR: Independent Local Radio.

in or **in cue**: The first few words of a tape or beginning of a record.

insert: A short live or recorded item in a programme, usually longer than a cut.

I/P: Input, where a signal enters a piece of equipment.

ips: Inches per second. The speed at which tape is travelling past the heads, usually 7½ ips for speech, and 15 ips for music (see **cps**).

IRN: Independent Radio News. The organisation which supplies national and international news to the ILR network.

jack plug: A connecting plug used to route or re-route sources and/or destinations. A 'mini-jack' is normally used on cassette machines.

jingle: Short musical piece used to identify the programme, station or, in advertising, the product.

key: A switch.

kilo: A thousand, as in kilohertz, the frequency in thousands of cycles per second.

lead: (a) The first, and most important, story in a bulletin or programme. (b) An electrical cable from one piece of equipment to another, e.g. a 'microphone lead', 'supply lead', etc.

leader or **leader tape**: Tape of the same width as recording tape which indicates the beginning of an item (usually green), the end of an item (usually red), or bands within an item (usually yellow).

LED: Light emitting diode. A meter consisting of lines of lights indicating loudness.

legals: (a) The potential dangers of running foul of legal constraints in libel, contempt, etc. (b) Checking a tape for those dangers.

level: (a) The measurement of volume being recorded. (b) A pre-recording check on a speaker's voice level, also known as 'level check' or 'taking some level'.

LF: (a) Low frequency, the bass sounds. (b) Long Wave transmissions.

line: A BT circuit for audio. A 'control line' gives about the quality of a telephone line, a 'music line' gives studio quality.

link: A cue between items, usually items on a similar subject.

live: Happening now, i.e. not recorded.

local end: A short distance circuit connecting a station to its nearest BT exchange.

log sheet: The sequence of ads which are decided by 'traffic'.

magnetic tape: Recording tape.

MCPS: Mechanical Copyright Protection Society. Licenses the reproduction of recorded sound.

MCR: Master Control Room. Where station output is usually monitored before being fed to the transmitter and where all outside sources are fed into and out again.

menu: Short tasters to indicate items to be covered in a programme.

MF: Medium frequency, or the Medium Wave transmitting band.

mike rattle: Noise on a recording due to the misuse of the microphone.

mix: The merging and balancing of two or more sounds or sources.

mixer: A piece of equipment with several sound channels which enables different sounds to be mixed.

modem: a device which can be connected to a computer to allow it to communicate with another computer on a telephone line (*mo*dulator/*dem*odulator).

mono: Single line sound source, as opposed to stereo.

mush: Tape interference that sounds similar to the wind.

music log: Details of music broadcast for calculation of PPL rates, PRS and needletime.

needletime: The allocated time for the use of commercial discs.

news agency: An organisation that compiles and distributes news stories, locally, nationally or internationally.

Newstar: A broadcasting computer system for reading and/or editing wire services and general word processing. The other common computer system is **Basys**.

OB: Outside broadcast.

off air: (a) Programme material heard or recorded from the radio. (b) General description for not being on-air, e.g. the off-air studio.

off mike: A speaker or noise either deliberately or accidentally not feeding directly into the microphone.

O/P: Output, where a signal emerges from a piece of equipment.

OP: 'Occasional programme' circuit. An ad-hoc booking through BT for a circuit between two studios.

open reel: A tape recorder with two reels or spools, a supply (or feeder) spool and a take-up spool. Used to differentiate from cassette and cartridge machines. Also called **reel-to-reel**.

Oracle: Independent television news and information text service on teletext TVs.

out: The last three words on a tape written as a warning that it is about to end.

out-times: the calculations in minutes and seconds for live speech to end so that the next item starts exactly on time, e.g. the on-hour news.

package: See **wrap**.

PA feed: A feed from the public address system at a conference where speakers will be using microphones running through it. Often requires special leads which need to be organised in advance.

para or **par**: Paragraph. As in 'Give me three short pars on that story'.

Parly: Parliament or IRN's Parliamentary unit; also extends to material from them, i.e. Parly wrap.

P as B: Programme as Broadcast. A written record of all the items broadcast on a particular programme. Also known as the log.

patch cord: A lead with jack plugs at each end.

patching: Using patch cords to re-direct sound sources on a jack field or patch panel.

phone-op: The person in charge of the switchboard, usually used for on-air phone-ins.

plug: Free advertisement, also known as a 'puff'.

popping: The sound of a sudden explosion of breath that results from being too close to the microphone, caused especially by words beginning with 'P' and 'B'.

pop-shield: See **windshield**.

pot: (a) End the transmission of a tape before the red leader. (b) Potentiometer: the volume control on a mixing desk channel.

PPL: Phonographic Performance Ltd. The organisation that licenses the broadcasting of sound recordings.

PPM: Peak Programme Meter. Indicates the loudness of audio material before it is transmitted.

PR: Public relations, or someone dealing with them (also **PRO**, Public Relations Office/Officer).

pre fade: The facility on mixing desks which allows a source to be heard before being faded up for transmission.

presser: A news conference.

prof: See **delay**. Also short for 'prof. button', which initiates prof.

promo: Promotional. See **trail**.

prospects: A list of the day's stories to be covered.

PRS: Performing Right Society. The organisation that collects royalties and redistributes the money to composers, publishers, performers, etc.

Q & A: Question and answer; an interview.

quarter track: Method of recording which splits the tape into four bands. Not usually used in professional recordings.

radio van or car: An OB vehicle capable of transmitting from the scene of a story to the studios.

reel: The spool onto which tape is wound, usually 5, 7, or 10.5 inches. The smaller sizes are referred to as cine spools, the 10.5 inch is called a NAB spool.

reel-to-reel: See **open reel**.

ROT: Recorded Off Transmission, also known as 'off-air check'.

rumble: A low frequency vibration caused by the turntable motor.

running order: A record of the order of items to be broadcast on a programme, and each of their durations.

running story: A developing story that keeps changing which needs constant revision and updates.

script: The written text for a broadcast.

seg or segue: To go from one piece of audio and/or music straight to another without linking script.

SOC: Standard Out Cue; e.g. 'Joe Bloggs, IRN, Madagascar'.

slug: See **catchline**.

source: (a) A supplier of news information or ideas. (b) The origin of audio material.

splash: Sound caused by over-sibilance, usually with words beginning 'S' or 'C', or equipment fault.

splice: The cutting and re-joining of tape. Hence 'splicing block' and 'splicing tape'.

spool: See **reel**.

sportsbox: Small portable mixer often used for coverage at sports grounds.

spot: (a) An advertisement. (b) An item regularly appearing in a programme, also known as 'fixed spot'.

sting: A short sequence of musical chords.

stringer: A freelance covering an area where there is no staff reporter available.

tail-ender: A light piece of news at the end of a programme or bulletin.

tail out or T/O: A tape that needs to be rewound before it can be played because it is on the reel backwards.

talk back: A communication system, either between control room and studio, or between adjacent studios, offices, etc.

TBU: Telephone Balancing Unit. Device to enable better quality two-way telephone reports or interviews.

teletext: TVs capable of showing Oracle and Ceefax.

tone: A signal used to synchronise levels between two sources.

tops: The higher frequency sounds of speech.

Tandy: A sort of lap-top portable personal computer, often used as a generic description. Used by reporters for filing copy to Newstar via a telephone modem.

top and tail: To attach leader tape against the first sound required on a recorded tape, to edit the tape, and then attach leader tape against the last sound required.

traffic: (a) The department that decides placement of ads on a log sheet according to each client's contract. (b) Reports on road traffic.

trail: A promotional 'spot' for a forthcoming programme. Also known as a 'promo'.

treble: High frequency sound waves.

TX: Transmission or transmitter.

UHF: Ultra High Frequency radio band.

update: A revised report with new information on a running story.

VHF: Very High Frequency band.

Vodaphone: A company operating a cellular radio telephone network. Often used as a generic term for the telephone itself.

voicer: A report using scripted copy read by a reporter or presenter without actuality.

vox pops: 'Voice of the people'. Reactions of people on the street edited together to provide a montage of opinions on a topic. Vox pops should not be presented as a representative sample.

VU: Volume Unit meter. Measures the average loudness of sound.

wavelength: The metered band used for tuning to a particular frequency.

wild track: Recording of the atmosphere on a location to be used as background noise later on.

windshield: A microphone cover, usually foam rubber, to protect against wind noise.

wipe: See **erase**.

wire services: National or international news gathering organisations which send stories by either teleprinter or computer.

wow: A recording fault which results in speed variations.

wrap: A report that includes more than one piece of actuality, linked by the reporter. Also known as a package or featurette.

1

Equipment

The operation of newsrooms and studios has changed dramatically since commercial radio went on air in 1973. Even as recently as five years ago, radio journalists had to try to concentrate amid the clattering of a room full of typewriters and wire service machines. Monitors had to be turned up loud enough to be heard over the din, and if you needed to speak to someone, tender tones were not the order of the day. It is hardly surprising that tempers flared.

Tempers still do erupt under the pressure of getting the news to air fast, but since computers entered the newsroom at least you know when people are angry and when they are just talking. The equipment is quieter, and every computer terminal has access to all the wire services without mountains of paper and noisy machines. It is comparative heaven.

Computers are not stopping at the newsroom. They will eventually amble into even the smallest studio, and then everything described here will be obsolete. But the new technology is still expensive, and re-equipping whole stations prohibitively so. It would be a brave person who tried to predict when the equipment and skills described here will be completely redundant.

Perhaps one day I will work in a station where there is no friction between the engineers and journalists, but it has not happened yet. Engineers complain that journalists do not know how to use the equipment and destroy anything they touch. Sometimes this is the result of sheer ignorance, but there have been flagrant cases of journalists taking their frustrations out on the machines. Generally my sympathy is with the engineers. Forget about doing your job well, you simply cannot do it at all without the machinery, so learn as much about it as possible and treat it with the respect it deserves.

Tape machines

There are three main sorts of tape recorders in use in most newsrooms: reel-to-reel (or open reel), portable (usually cassette machines) and cartridge.

Professional reel-to-reel tape machines (and some cassette machines) have three 'heads' – the small metal rectangles that convert electric pulses onto or off tape. These are erase, record and playback. They appear in that order (reading left to right), because logic dictates that the tape is first erased, to allow the recording, which is then played back. If the machine is not in record mode, the first two heads are simply by-passed.

When you are recording and wearing headphones to check the sound, you listen off the record head. This is because the space between the two heads, though very slight, is enough to create a small delay that the brain cannot accommodate. Try a little experiment: set a machine to listen off playback in your headphones and then recite 'Mary had a little lamb'. The odds are that you will not get past the third word.

In cassette and cartridge machines the record and playback heads are usually combined so there is no delay. Also note that cartridge machines do not have erase heads (see p. 31).

The heads of recorders are very complex and sensitive. They should be protected, cleaned regularly and carefully maintained so they stay aligned and work well.

When tape is laced up on any tape machine, it will go around a guide pillar just before the heads, across the heads, then past a capstan and pressure roller before being wound round the take-up spool on the right. When the machine is switched on, the pressure roller pushes against the capstan, which brings the tape up against the heads.

There are three sizes of spools for open reel machines: 5, 7 and 10.5 inches. Different sized spools require the machines to run on different 'tensions', i.e. how much pull or drag the feed (left) and take-up (right) spools exert. Machines can be switched from one size to another, and you will find the machine will not work properly if you select the wrong one. Machines also get confused if you mix the sizes of the spools, say if you have a 5″ on the left spool and a 10.5″ on the right, so be sure to use the same size on both.

Different sized reels have different centres. 5″ and 7″ have 'cine' centres, which look like an x in the middle, and 10.5″ have 'NAB' centres. NAB stands for the National Association of Broadcasters, and is the organisation which monitors professional standards and procedures in the US. NAB spools have a hole in the centre approximately 3″ in diameter, with 3 little half-moon arcs on the outside. There are 10.5″ spools with cine centres, but they are rare. Most tapes that eventually get to air are on NAB spools, so the machines must have 'NAB adaptors' or centres for the tapes to fit on.

The speed of a tape is measured by how fast it moves across the heads, and the two speeds used most often on open reels are 7.5 inches per second (19 cm per second) and 15 ips (38 cps). 7.5 ips is the norm for speech, 15 ips for music. You can do a very rough calculation of, say, how much has been edited out of a tape by estimating how many inches have been taken out. Fifteen inches would be two seconds at 7.5 ips.

The faster the tape moves across the heads, the better the sound quality. This is because magnetic tape always creates 'tape hiss', but the heads read higher frequencies better at higher speeds.

A 5″ reel of tape will hold just over 15 minutes of recording capacity at 7.5 ips, a 7″ about half an hour, and a 10.5″ around one hour and 10 minutes.

Cassette machines use tape which is only ⅛ of an inch wide and operate at a speed of just 1⅞ ips, which means that the quality is not as good as reel-to-reel, even though modern technology has improved them to such an extent that most of us do not have sensitive enough hearing to tell the difference. The cost, weight and compact nature of cassette machines mean they are more the norm for radio reporters than reel-to-reel portables. Their disadvantage is that you cannot directly edit the tapes.

The cassette machines used most often these days are the Marantz and the Sony Walkman Professional.

The Marantz is a professional American-made machine which includes a feature that allows for some speed variation – a life-saver if the batteries begin to die just as the interview gets good.

The size and weight of the Sony Pro speak for themselves, but Sonys are rarely company issue because they are not as robust as the Marantz. Some reporters decide to invest in them personally. If you do this, be careful in your choice of microphone. Since reporters deal mainly in the spoken word, a stereo mike is unnecessary, but be sure to choose one that is of broadcast standard. An AKG D160, for example, would stand you in good stead.

The one drawback to the Sony Pro is that its output level has a fairly limited gain, so there may be a problem when you are trying to feed down a poor-quality telephone line.

Cassettes come in various lengths, but most reporters are issued with C60s, which allow 30 minutes of recording on each side.

If reel-to-reel portables are found in a newsroom, they will almost certainly be Uhers (pronounced 'you-ers'). These are German, battery-operated machines which conform to professional standards, can take a lot of knocking about (an essential feature for a day-to-day reporter), and are very useful for 'on the job' editing. But, apart from the fact that they cost more than cassette machines, they are also heavy (more than 20 lbs without batteries and carrying case), and cannot take tape spools of more than 5″, which is just over 15 minutes' recording time at 7.5 ips.

The other professional portable that you may see is the

Swiss-made Nagra. Its technical specifications are so good that this little machine, even though it is smaller and lighter than a Uher, is almost equivalent to having a good quality studio slung over your shoulder. It is a fantastic machine, but it is also fantastically expensive.

One other sort of tape machine is found in newsrooms – the cartridge, or cart machine. Short news cuts, station jingles or inserts for packages are better recorded on carts, because they are fast and flexible. Carts work on a single loop of tape of varying lengths, and when a cart is being recorded the machine puts an inaudible pulse at the start of the recording (the 'cue pulse'). The machine will automatically stop the cart at the pulse so that it is cued at the beginning of the recording and ready for air. Cart machines, however, do not have erase heads, so they must always be bulk-erased (see p. 35) before you record onto them, and you must always play back your recordings to ensure you did not start with a 'dirty' cart.

That will also bring home the importance of using the correct length cart in the first place. You have to wait until the cue pulse stops the cart before you can take it out of the machine, so if you have put a 15″ report on a 100″ cart, you'll be twiddling your thumbs for a while. One of the most usual mistakes made in busy newsrooms is that carts are stopped before they have got to their cue pulse, which means that when that cart is next played on air, only silence comes out. Always let the cart play through.

Most cart machines have a *fast forward* button. If it is pressed the cue pulse will be found at fast speed. You can also initiate the fast forward capability automatically by incorporating an additional pulse at the end of the recorded item.

The choice of functions on tape and cassette machines is pretty much the same regardless of type. *Rewind* and *fast forward* buttons are usually on their respective ends, embracing *play* and *record*, and sometimes *pause* and/or *edit*. If a machine has the *edit* option, it must be pressed before you can hear the tape for editing.

Some machines give you a *tape dump* option, which

means the tape is fed through by the tension of the capstan and roller alone, and the right-hand spool does not turn. This option is also designed for editing, usually of longer segments.

Most machines require both the *record* and *play* buttons to be pressed at the same time in order to start recording. 'Spooling through' a tape refers to when you are in *rewind* or *fast forward*.

If you are editing on a machine that has the *safe* option, use it to ensure that you do not accidentally start recording over the tape that is being edited.

Recording tape

All these machines use magnetic tape, which is a specially treated strip of plastic. Usually the back of the tape is dull, while the magnetic side is glossy. The magnetic side is coated with iron oxide and records electronic pulses off the record head according to the frequency and amplitude of the sound sent to the head. The iron oxide coating is damaged a little each time the tape is recorded on, or played back, and tapes can get 'oxidised', which means they are worn out. If a tape is oxidised, it begins to sound as though it was recorded underwater. Always destroy oxidised tape so that it does not find its way back into the system, destroying someone else's brilliant recording.

Recording tape is always ¼″ wide, but its thickness varies. If it is 1¼ mil (mil = one thousandth of an inch) thick, it is called 'long play' tape. This is because, since it is so thin, you can wind more onto the spool. That is about its only positive attribute, though. It is difficult to handle because it stretches so easily, and your recording can be distorted or destroyed simply by fast spooling if the tension on the machine is too great for the tape to withstand. It is also difficult to edit, because unless you are working with virtually a new blade, it will tend to be stretched rather than cut.

The thickness of the tape that is generally used is 2 mils or 'standard play' tape.

Recording tape is often *reclaimed*, i.e. bits of tapes that have already been used are spliced and wound together to be used again. Stations usually have a policy about how long the bits need to be before they can be reclaimed, because 'slash' tape, as it is also sometimes called, should not have too many splices in it. Tapes are candidates for reclamation only if they are at least 10 or 15 minutes long.

Video tape can be used to record sound only, and the quality is much better than recording tape. However, those ILR stations that are equipped to use video recorders only use them as logging machines to retain the station's output for up to three months.

Leader tape

In order to show where the actual recording starts and ends, and to allow the tape to be 'lined up' on the studio tape recorder so that it is ready to start at just the right place and time, you splice on *leader tape*.

Leader is the same width as the recording tape, i.e. ¼'', but it is pure plastic and coloured. House styles vary, but usually green leader is attached to the front of a mono tape, red leader always at the back. If a tape is 'banded', and has a series of actuality bits that need to be linked, the bands are separated with yellow leader. Different sorts of recording modes are also indicated by putting different coloured leader on the front, e.g. white for half-track, or red-and-white striped for stereo recordings.

Leader tape should be spliced tight up against the start (or end) of the audio so it can be used as an accurate visual guide.

Do not get carried away with leader tape. There needs to be enough of it to be able to get a firm bite when it is being lined up in the studio, but four feet is certainly sufficient. Miles of leader on the front of a tape can add crucial seconds to getting the tape ready for air if there happens to be a panic on. Similarly, use enough yellow leader so that bands can be spotted visually, but not so much that it takes longer to line up the band than it takes to read the link.

Twelve to eighteen inches of banding leader will usually be about right.

Meters and levels

Equipment carries meters to help you keep sound levels within prescribed limits. If levels fluctuate too much, the listener will certainly get fed up with having to adjust the volume control. Levels also need to be controlled for technical reasons. If the level is too low for a sustained period of time, the transmitter will try to find some sound to boost artificially, while if levels go too high, the sound becomes distorted and difficult to understand. But equipment meters are really only there as a back-up – because the most important meters are your ears. If the recording is 'compressed' so that the upper and lower ranges of sounds are forced into the middle range, as most ads are, your ears will tell you to peak lower. If it is a 'thin' telephone line (e.g. when the line is not carrying the bass range leaving only the less forceful treble sounds), you will go over the guide limits.

There are three sorts of meters on equipment: VU (volume unit), PPM (peak programme meter), and LED (light emitting diode).

VU meters show the average recording or playback levels rather than the peaks, and you tend to find them on cheaper equipment. The peak level is '0', and above that the meter literally goes into the red.

PPM meters measure the high peaks of sound, but they do not fall back instantly, making them easier to use than VUs. Sounds should normally peak at between 4 and 6 for speech, but check the particular station's policy.

LED meters are more dependable and less expensive than either of the other two. They consist of rows of lights which change colour from yellow to red. As with VUs, you should only get slightly into the red in the loudest parts.

Bulk erasers

Bulk erasers are very strong electromagnets which destroy all the magnetic patterns made by recording on an entire tape. All old carts and reclaimed tape should be bulk-erased.

In the days before digital watches, a lot of heart-rending mistakes were made at the bulk eraser. That expensive little timepiece that was a present last Christmas would be irrevocably welded into a magnetised lump, never to work again. The field of the eraser is larger than just its surface, depending on the size and power of the eraser. If you still wear a mechanical watch, be sure to keep it well away (say 2 feet to be absolutely certain) or somewhere the field cannot penetrate (like your back pocket). That also applies to anything in any way dependent on magnetics, including the magnetic coding strip on bank and credit cards!

Do not, whatever you do, leave a tape you want anywhere near a bulk eraser. Even if it is not completely wiped, the extended field of the eraser can affect a strip through the entire tape, leaving regular drop-outs and making the tape un-broadcastable. Some erasers are specifically designed to bulk-erase carts and therefore look very much like cart machines. Be sure you know the difference!

If a tape is badly bulk-erased, a sort of whooshing noise will run through its entire length. To bulk-erase tape properly, it should be turned on the surface of the eraser in the same direction as it is wound on the spool, continuing the motion as the tape is taken off the eraser. The exercise is repeated in the other direction once the tape has been turned over. You will get the whooshes if you leave tape motionless on the eraser.

Studio equipment

Most main control rooms have at least two open reel tape recorders, a cart '3 stack' (i.e. a machine which will hold three carts to be used in succession or mixed together but only has the capacity to playback), a record cart machine, two record turntables, and a CD player. All this equipment is wired into a 'mixing desk'.

The mixing desk has more than one 'channel', or source of sound, and is either operated by an engineer or 'self-opped' by the presenter. Which channel is heard is decided by which faders are open. If there is more than one fader up, then sounds are being mixed together in some way. It could be as simple as two microphones being faded up for an interview, or it could be some combination of all the other equipment available, like music from one of the turntables being mixed with a pre-recorded sound-track off one of the tape machines, and a reporter talking over both.

Control rooms are laid out so that whoever is operating the desk can easily reach the equipment, with the ads, which will usually be on carts, arranged numerically in a cart rack.

Main control rooms are linked with a studio, and the two sides look at each other through a specially sound-proofed window. They speak to each other through a system known as 'talk-back' which allows the control-room to speak to the presenter without being heard either on the tape that is being recorded or on air during live programmes. The presenter can also speak to the control-room but, obviously, only when the microphone is not on.

Studios are usually organised around some sort of round table with microphone leads fed through a hole in the centre. Presenters sit on the side of the table that commands the best view of the control room, while guests often have their backs to it. Apart from the obvious advantages of this arrangement, it is sometimes helpful for the guest to be unable to see the producer or engineer, who will often indicate visually that the interview is boring and should be wound up.

Recording booths

Most stations in the ILR network broadcast a combination of music and talk, and their recording booths generally contain two turntables, one tape machine, a cart stack, and a mixing desk with a smaller capacity than the desk in the main control rooms. If booths have been designed to record only interviews (like most of the booths attached to news operations), they will not have any turntables.

Booths are designed as 'self-op' areas, which means the journalist or DJ rather than an engineer controls the equipment. They are only large enough for one or two people.

Field equipment

When a recording is being made in a studio, its quality should be assured because it is being made in controlled, professional surroundings. Once you are out in the field, however, it is up to you and your equipment to keep up the quality.

The simplest field work requires just a portable cassette machine, a microphone and a cassette, but good reporters carry some additional equipment with them at all times. No self-respecting reporter would ever leave base without spare batteries and at least one spare cassette.

Crocodile clips, or 'croc' clips, are the traditional way to send a recording down the telephone from the output channel of the tape machine. Strictly speaking, this practice is against British Telecom regulations unless you are using a BT-approved device. In any case, the use of croc clips is becoming very limited as more phones become vandal-resistant or, worse, moulded bits of plastic. You have got to be able to unscrew the mouthpiece and disconnect one wire in order to attach the clips.

A piece of equipment frequently used by reporters to enhance telephone quality is a small battery-operated unit manufactured by Comrex. The output of a cassette machine or a microphone is plugged into the input of the Comrex and the output is then connected to the telephone line, either by croc clips or through the connector box. While the Comrex is in 'by-pass' mode a normal conversation can take place, but when the audio is to be fed the by-pass switch is de-activated. Whenever the by-pass is de-activated, the person who is speaking will sound like a character out of a Disney film talking under water unless the receiving unit is switched on. That's because most of the noise that makes listening to telephone quality most annoying is in the lower frequencies, and what the Comrex does is to lift the sounds out of those low frequencies. The receiver then translates the audio back into a normal listening formulation without all the low-frequency noise.

The introduction of cellular radio telephones has been a god-send. The newsdesk can be in permanent contact with a reporter, and a story can be filed from anywhere, so long as the batteries hold up. But be sure to disable the telephone's ringing capability while doing an interview! Some cellular phones have been adapted to accept the output of a tape recorder or lap-top personal computer.

Portable computers have changed the face of field work. Parts of the ILR network use a computer called Newstar which is specially designed for broadcasting. If a reporter is equipped with a light-weight portable computer compatible with the Newstar computer at base, cues and copy stories can be sent directly to the station via a modem. Without a pc, you must go through the time-consuming process of reading the information down a telephone for someone at base to type up.

2

Using the equipment

Recording

If you are in a self-op booth doing an interview, either with someone on the phone (a phone-out) or across the desk from you, you must keep an eye on the level and a hand on the fader in order to 'ride the levels' and keep them right.

If it is a phone-out, you will get much better quality if you dip the phone fader when you are asking a question, because the phone line will 'colour' your voice and make it sound odd. The phone fader does not need to go all the way down; how far you need to compensate will depend on the desk and the line, so use your ears. Obviously you must take your mike fader all the way out if you want to clear your throat or make any other noise.

If you are doing an interview down the telephone, it is an IBA regulation that you must make it absolutely clear to the interviewee that you are recording the conversation for possible use on air!

If the interviewee is across the desk from you, learn how to keep a peripheral eye on the meter without losing eye contact with the guest. Some people will be put off if you seem obsessed with the equipment.

If guests kick the table while crossing their legs, or have a habit of tapping the desk to emphasise a point, great thumps will come through on the recording, and those points will need to be gone over again without the thumps. The most magnificent thumps are made by accidentally bumping the mike itself. Don't worry, your deafness is only temporary.

The reason you are deaf, of course, is because you are wearing headphones, which you must do whenever you are doing anything in any studio. The headphones, or 'cans', give you an accurate reflection of what is happening on the recording or on air; your ears can lie to you, or simply not hear as much as the microphone picks up. If you are involved in anything live on air, talk-back from the control room will go into the cans even when the mike is on, so it is the fastest way a producer or engineer can communicate with you.

When you are recording out in the field you will not be wearing cans, so your ears must be sensitive to the atmosphere you are working in and to any extraneous sounds that could make editing the tape impossible, or become acutely annoying to the listener. If, for example, you are doing an interview and a plane flies overhead, you will not be able to edit the material recorded over the plane noise because it will be noticeable to the listener. And if an important point the listener should hear is being made during all this, forget it. The listener's concentration will be focussed on the plane. The noise may actually make a point in itself if the interview is about the level of noise planes make: excellent reports were filed when residents near Heathrow were complaining about the amount of noise Concorde made – and the interviews just had to stop when it took off. But keep your ears open for sounds you do not want, interrupt the interview, apologise to the inverviewee, try to put him or her at ease again, and then ask the last question again.

If you are recording in a busy street, you will have to get the microphone as close to the interviewees as possible in order to have more of them than traffic noise. Watch your recording levels: you will have to bring them right down to compensate for being so close. Make similar allowances when recording in large rooms with high ceilings and bare floors. They tend to be natural echo-chambers and are jarring to the listener when the recording is dropped into a studio-quality programme. If there are curtains or anything else that will absorb some of the reverberations, do the interview in that part of the room, but still be conscious of working with the microphone closer to the interviewee than normal. That way you will make the mike concentrate on the voice, not the echo.

If you are using a machine with an automatic level control (ALC), you are best advised not to use it. When ALC is switched on, the machine will automatically bring up any sound it can find to the peak level, including background noises while someone is taking a breath or considering a point. Apart from the fact that it sounds odd to the listener, this, too, can make editing difficult.

Whenever you are using a portable tape machine, be extra careful with the mike lead. The vulnerable bits are where it comes out of the machine and into the mike itself. If the lead on either of those ends wobbles around you will get 'mike rattle' – clicks and thumps that obliterate the noise you wanted to record. Be sure that the lead coming out of the machine will not bump against anything, and then loop the lead at the other end around your hand so that the lead does not move back and forth as you move the microphone. Grip it firmly, but do not let the lead rub against the mike – that produces a squelch of its own.

Most important of all, remember that without your machinery you cannot do your job, so treat your cassette machine like any other piece of valuable property. Don't lose it, loan it, or leave it lying around!

Dubbing

If your interview is on cassette, it will have to be dubbed before it can be edited and go to air. A dub, derived from 'double', is a copy of any source to any other. You will need a lead with the correct sort of plugs to fit into the out channel of your machine and the input of the machine or desk you are dubbing to or through. While you are dubbing, watch your levels and keep your ears open to monitor quality.

You will also save youself time if you 'flag' the main part of the tape you want in the final version. That means either making a note of where it is after you have zeroed the

physically popping a very small scrap of paper
e as it is going onto the take-up spool. If you have
ew that is ridiculously longer than required, only
dub o... ose sections that are going to make it into the final
version.

Editing

Editing tape is a knack we all have to learn. Everybody is
all thumbs to start with, and it is only through practice that
it becomes a skill that can be performed well, even under
intense pressure of time. You will eventually be able to edit
out 's' at the end of a word, take whole questions and
answers from one part of the tape and insert them
somewhere else, or pretty much whatever you want to do –
all without anybody being able to tell you have touched the
tape.

But be careful that you *never* change the meaning of
what is said, omit qualifications to statements or
comments, or edit material to give the impression of a
conversation going on, or answers being given, to questions
put in other interviews.

It is only the very exceptional tape that goes to air
without some edits. The purposes of editing are:

- To get rid of unwanted material. Whether it is to bring
  an eight-minute interview down to four, or cleaning up
  pauses or stammers.
- To rearrange the order. The answers to questions four
  and six may both be interesting and worthy of being left
  in, but if answer number six is more newsworthy, it
  should come before answer four.

There are several different ways to edit a tape: the splice
cut, the cross-record, and the computer-controlled edit.
Very few newsrooms are sophisticated enough to have
computer editing, and cross-recording, which involves
using a precise playback machine and an operator with
nifty co-ordination, is usually engineer-controlled. The

most common form of editing is the trusty old splice cut.

You need an open reel tape machine with exposed heads, a splicing block, a chinagraph pencil, a single-edged razor blade and splicing tape.

A splicing block has a groove down the middle which is fractionally less than the width of ¼'' tape, and there are two or three vertical slots across it at different angles. The block holds the tape securely so that a precision cut can be made.

A chinagraph, or grease pencil, is used to mark where a tape is to be cut. Since that mark is made while the tape is stretched across the playback head, a pen, ordinary pencil or the like should *never* be used. A well-sharpened chinagraph will make a precise mark without damaging the head.

The procedure involves locating the beginning of the material that is not wanted on the tape, marking it while it is sitting on the playback head, moving on through the tape until you get to the beginning of material that needs to stay in the tape, and then marking that. The first mark is placed on the splicing block and cut through the 45° angle slot. Follow the same procedure for the second mark. The unwanted bit of tape is now gone.

The two ends are then butted together in the groove of the block. There should be no gap at all between them, nor should they overlap, even by a fraction. A short length of splicing tape is cut from the roll, usually 2'' or less, and pressed firmly over the two ends. The splicing tape must be exactly positioned on the tape so that no sticky bits are left exposed. If they are, the excess must be trimmed while the edit is in the block. Sloppy applications of splicing tape will stop a tape from going over the heads, which could pose more than a small problem during a live programme.

To locate the place on the tape that needs to be marked, stop the machine at about the right place, then manually move the spools backwards or forwards until the exact place is on the playback head. It sometimes helps if you mumble along with the words on the tape, because that assists in breaking down words, even letters, so that you do not accidentally cut off the end or beginning of a word. You will find it easier to edit words that begin with a 'hard' or 'explosive' letter, such as b, d, p, s and t.

A good rule of thumb is to mark the first sound *after* a breath. Never edit out all the breaths, because it would be unnatural for anyone to speak that way. What you are trying to do is to rid the tape of material without the listener being able to tell that anything has been removed.

A common mistake beginners make is to move the tape so slowly that the words no longer flow at a recognisable rate. Move the tape at as close to the right speed as possible – that makes it easier to find the correct spot to mark.

Never throw away the bit of tape you have edited out until you have listened back to check that it is a good edit.

The reason we use the 45° angle is because it gives a stronger bond. Cutting the tape weakens it, and using the longer angle spreads the weakness. If an edit is very tight, the 60° or 90° angle can be used, but if you are having to consider that, you should also consider whether this is one of those rare times when a particular edit is just not possible. The 90° angle is also used in editing music as the edits need to be made between beats and therefore require that degree of precision.

A stronger edit can also be achieved if the two ends are butted next to each other on a section of the block that does not have an angled slot. When you press down on the splicing tape, you will find that it does not adhere to the little space made by the slot, and therefore creates a weak spot.

Never use miles of splicing tape. Apart from the fact that long, gangling bits are difficult to position precisely, once the tape gets archived it is the sticky bit of the tape which eventually deteriorates. It may be possible to work around short bits of tape, but not wodges. It is not the length of splicing tape that makes a secure edit, but the precision of the whole process.

Studio discipline

Studio discipline is important because it is not possible to create a good radio programme without all those involved in it hearing it. If the presenter does not hear the pre-recorded tapes, it is not possible to engage the skill of integrating them into a whole programme. If a producer is not listening to a live interview, there is no way of knowing whether all the pertinent points have been covered. And so on.

So the first rule of studio discipline is silence. Be sure that the things that need to be said are clearly understood, and then shut up. Never shout: it is inevitably a sign of panic.

If you do have information that needs to be imparted, be sensitive with your timing. Do not, whatever you do, distract the engineer when an 'out' cue is imminent or unnecessarily distract a presenter by using talk-back during a live interview.

Guests should only be allowed into a control room when the producer or the engineer agrees, and they must speak in voices low enough to allow the team to keep listening to the programme. Otherwise ask them to leave.

When it comes to decisions, the second rule of studio discipline is that it is the producer who makes them. The engineer may question the broadcast quality of a phone line or a recording, but the producer decides whether the story is big enough to warrant inflicting it on the listener. The presenter may suggest changes to the order in which items are to go out, but the producer decides.

The reasoning behind this rule is simple. If there is anarchy on a programme, that is what the listener will hear, so one person has got to make the final decisions, and those decisions must be made clear to everyone concerned and accepted even if they are wrong.

Profanity

'Profanity', or prof, is the term generally used for a delayed broadcast. British Telecom requires any station that runs phone-ins to have a delay system 'available', but it does not insist that it is used. The IBA recommends that all phone-ins or programmes that let members of the public on air should be 'in profanity'.

The way prof works is as follows. The output of the live programme is sent from the studio to a piece of equipment called a digital delay unit. This prevents the programme from being fed to the transmitter for up to ten seconds, so that if anyone swears, libels someone, commits contempt, or whatever, the producer or presenter in the live studio can press the prof button, and a jingle will be played to air instead of the offending remark.

Nowadays the delay is always achieved by digital techniques, but the principle may be easier to grasp if we consider the old-fashioned system. The live programme was sent to a tape machine which was re-designed so that after the programme had been recorded on the record head, the tape went on a wander, being fed back and forth over extra guide posts, before eventually finding its way back to the playback head ten seconds after it was recorded. It was what went over the playback head that was sent to the transmitter and therefore what the listener heard.

With either system, the delay gap must be filled at the beginning of the programme while the machinery delays the broadcast. That gap is filled by inserting either the same jingle that will over-ride any offensive remark, or a special one.

Let's take the example of the *Brian Hayes Programme*. At the beginning of the programme, Alan Clark reads the national and international news sequence, then the ad sequence. If you are in Brian's studio, the next thing you hear is him saying 'Good morning London', but if you are outside the studio, you hear the ads and then a sting, before Brian's 'Good Morning London'. The programme is now in delay.

The programme has to come out of delay at the end of each hour, so the studio will have to hear 10 seconds of the programme twice. For example, if there is an ad break going up to the top of the hour, the studio will hear the whole of the last ad live in the studio, then switch the monitor to listen to the programme from the transmitter, thus hearing the last 10 seconds of the ad again, before pressing the button to come out of prof.

3

Responsibilities, Objectivity and Confidentiality

Reporting events, whether local or international, is one of the most important services any radio station provides. Even if the main format of a station is music-based, people depend on the radio to tell them what is happening when a major story breaks. Its flexibility and immediacy make radio the perfect medium for fast-breaking news. This is a big advantage, but it is also a responsibility. It is a responsibility which, quite rightly, is mainly carried by us – the broadcasters. The government can, and has, stepped in to stop particular programmes (e.g. *My Country Right or Wrong*), and this country does have more legal constraints than most, but we still do operate a so-called 'free press'. The government does not tell us what to report or how, so it is up to us to be sure that we deserve the listener's confidence.

Lord Donaldson, giving his judgment in the *Spycatcher* Appeal in February 1988, gave a pretty good definition of journalism: '... the media are the eyes and ears of the general public. They act on behalf of the general public. Their right to know and their right to publish is neither more nor less than that of the general public. Indeed it is that of the general public for whom they are trustees.' He then went on to say that no one could publish anything from Peter Wright's book, but the relevant point here is that while journalists have to be vigilant on behalf of the public, they do not have any special rights enshrined in law to carry out that vigilance.

What is news?

News = new, interesting, true

My paraphrase of Robert McLeish's definition of news captures the essence of what news stories must contain and convey. News must also be informative and relevant. A story may be interesting, but does it matter to the listener? Even if a story is complicated and difficult to explain in a few sentences, it is your job to find the right words and make the story relevant to your listener.

Every item you send to air must get all the facts right, because the listener is depending on you and has no way of checking on what you have said. If it turns out that what you have reported is wrong in any way, the listener will not believe anything else you report later on. That loss of trust affects not just you but the entire station, so be sure to get all the details right, including names, initials, titles and figures.

Speaking of figures, remember the old dictum that they can be made to say anything: make their meaning clear. Be especially careful with percentages, which must be put in context. A large percentage increase in crime in a given area is meaningless if the boundaries of that area have changed since the last figures were compiled.

If at any time you are not sure of a fact, the rule is *return to source*. If you are writing up some information for use on air and realise you have not made a complete note of the details you need to include, pick up the phone and find out. If that is not possible, you should attribute or qualify the facts in the story.

If for some reason that is not possible, the other golden rule is *if in doubt, leave it out*. This is a phrase you will often hear in newsrooms because it is basic to the job. Part of a journalist's responsibilities is to get across new and important information, but if for any reason you are not absolutely sure that something is right, it's better not to run it at all.

There are a lot of golden rules in radio and in journalism,

but 'return to source' and 'if in doubt, leave it out' are particularly important because if you adhere to them you will never lie to the listener.

Objectivity

Tony Benn has been known to point out to interviewers that he was elected, while they were not. Even if the interviewer is asking a question the elector might well have put had it been possible, Mr Benn has a point. The listener has selected you, not elected you. Those who take decisions over our lives have been elected on the basis of their opinions and promises. You don't take those sorts of decisions, and your opinions are irrelevant.

That you think carefully about what you do is obviously important, but your job is to present facts and other people's opinions in an objective way so that the listener can make up his or her own mind. Objectivity is an important concept in journalism but difficult to achieve in practice. To be truly objective we would need to divorce ourselves from our backgrounds and prejudices. There is a long-standing debate about whether this is possible, but you should at least know your own prejudices and confine them to a part of your mind that becomes inoperative when you are doing your job. You will find it easier to interview people who do not hold the same views as you do, simply because you will be able to think of the opposing arguments more quickly. Remember that it is always your job to find the opposite point of view and put it. There are very few one-sided issues. If for some reason you are forced to give only one side of a story, you owe it to the listener to explain why.

There are problematic areas, of course. For instance, is that person carrying a gun a 'terrorist' or a 'freedom fighter'? Often the solution is to use only strictly accurate terms. A station I worked for in the States during the Vietnam war, for example, had a house rule that all reports should use the terms 'North Vietnamese' or 'NFL' rather than 'Vietcong'. That was because the term 'Vietcong', an amalgamation of Vietnamese and communist, was an invention of the American forces, so in the interest of objectivity and accuracy, we did not use it.

But there are times when objectivity is not possible. In the reporting of events in Northern Ireland, in order to 'starve the terrorist of the oxygen of publicity', the Home Secretary has banned us from broadcasting any statement made by anyone sympathetic to the aims of certain organisations, even if that person is an elected councillor representing one of those organisations (see p. 182). This makes it very difficult to present objective reports.

I have emphasised the importance of presenting facts and opinions so that the listener can form a fair assessment, but there are times when the listener does not expect objectivity. When stories are difficult to report because of their social context, stand back and think about what the listener would consider right and wrong. In coverage of Northern Ireland, it would not be socially acceptable for reports to seem to condone terrorism even if they pass a purely objective test. There were disagreements about the coverage of the Zeebrugge ferry disaster: did the media intrude on people's grief, were the descriptions of what happened in the ship too graphic, should reports include details of the state of corpses being taken out of the water? While some of these questions overlap with those of good taste, they also have to do with objective considerations of how much of the story to tell and how much to leave out.

You will sometimes have to decide whether to report on an issue that the majority of people might well put into the 'wrong' category. In the late 1970s, would you have opted for the argument that the National Front should not be given air time because their views are racist and an incitement to prejudice, or for the view that they should be given enough rope to hang themselves? (There are laws against incitement to racial hatred, and if you had opted for the second argument, you would have had to lose your objectivity if a discussion began to stray into an area that contravened the law.)

It is generally accepted that democracy works on the basis of society making moral, political and social decisions in an atmosphere of free debate. It is part of our job to present the debate, but from as neutral a standpoint as possible.

Confidentiality

Journalists use the phrase 'the right to know' frequently, and quite rightly. This country has more legal restrictions on reporting than almost any other, but within those bounds it is our job to keep important facts and issues in the public arena.

It is a journalist's job to uncover and report on issues that some might prefer did not become public, and it is not unusual for the courts to become involved in the tussle of deciding whether certain stories should be told, and by whom. Traditionally, journalists do not 'reveal their sources', and some reporters and editors have been fined or even jailed for upholding that tradition.

The 1981 Contempt of Court Act was the first statute to give reporters some protection for concealing sources, unless a court decides that 'disclosure is necessary in the interest of justice or national security, or for the prevention of disorder or crime.' Unfortunately some cases have shown that the courts are taking a very broad view of these exceptions. Even though each case is decided on its own merits, it is possible that the Act will not give as much protection as some had hoped.

The 1984 Police and Criminal Evidence Act offers journalists some protection for confidentiality with one hand, but takes it away with the other. While part of the Act protects 'journalistic material' and gives reporters the opportunity to argue in court against having to reveal information that has been collected, another section allows police to search for and seize material by applying to a circuit judge for a warrant.

Generally the law of confidentiality, as it is broadly known, is used not to protect or help journalists, but to stop them publishing particular kinds of information. Thus the courts will protect facts that have been obtained by someone in confidential circumstances. This has traditionally been used to stop employees or former employees from divulging a company's secrets.

The law has recently been extended, however, notably in the *Spycatcher* case in which the courts agreed with the government's argument that Peter Wright, along with all former security service employees, has a life-long duty of confidentiality. The Australian courts did not agree, so, even though the government fought to prevent it, publication of *Spycatcher* went ahead there. There was no attempt to prevent publication in the US, possibly because of the provisions of the Constitution. This duty of confidentiality has now been written into the new Official Secrets Act.

Good taste

News is often 'bad news', and journalists often end up reporting the unsavoury side of life. This is where considerations of 'good taste' come in.

A few years ago, a petrol tanker crashed and exploded in a holiday camping area in Spain. The IRN reporter sent to cover the story told me off-air that he was finding it difficult to keep his stomach because of the pervasive smell of burned flesh. Would it have been an appropriate fact to include in the report? He left it out as the story was horrific enough without that particular embellishment.

Stories that involve disasters can cause a lot of distress to the listener. If there has been an earthquake or a plane crash involving large numbers of people, we all have a moment's fear, wondering whether anyone we know is involved. You can reduce some of the distress by giving as much information as you can as soon as you can.

When the Clapham rail crash story first broke, anyone who knew someone who was, or might have been, travelling by rail at about the time of the crash would have been worried about them. When we started getting details of which trains were involved, where they had been travelling from, and so on, at least some listeners' fears could be put to rest. Ask yourself what questions the listener is asking, then answer them early on in the report. This is not just good taste, it is also good journalism.

Be conscious of the dangers of causing offence. Sex, race and religion are supposed to be taboo subjects at dinner parties, because someone is bound to offend someone else. They cannot be taboo on the air, but think about how and why you are describing someone. Not all black people are immigrants, not all Jewish people are Zionists. And in either case, is the label relevant to the story?

If the story involves sex, don't be salacious or squalid. Choose your words as if you were at that dinner party, talking to people you do not know very well and do not want to offend. Use proper or medical terms when you can, remembering that the listener will need to understand them.

Finally, you will be accused of bad taste if you place inappropriate items next to one another. To use an extreme example, do not follow the Clapham rail crash story with one about new excursion fares for holiday-makers. The listener's sensibilities will be bruised. Be aware of which ads are running. Most stations operate a policy of pulling related ads off air if there is a major story running. It is simply bad taste to report the horrors of a major air crash and follow it with a chirpy jingle extolling the virtues of an airline. The advertisers not only understand this policy, they encourage it. The ads can be re-scheduled to run later when they will not be offensive.

Complaints

The IBA says there is a danger of increasing acrimony if an angry caller is put through directly to someone involved in the programme that is the subject of the complaint, but sometimes there is no real choice. There is always a temptation to dismiss the complaint, either mentally or verbally, as trivial and only the view of one listener. Don't.

If a listener is already annoyed enough to ring, and you act in an off-hand manner, you may lose that listener forever. The listener heard what you had to say, now it is your turn to listen.

You can often deal with a complaint either by explaining why something was done in a particular way, or listening politely to the complaint and then giving an assurance that the point has been taken. After all, sometimes listeners *do* make good points. If you have made a mistake, apologise and assure the listener that steps will be taken to ensure it will not happen again (and then take those steps).

On the other hand, do not let the listener dictate editorial policy. If a demand is made for 'equal time' or 'right of reply', deal with it sensitively but firmly. If you are not getting anywhere, ask the person to write. That not only gives you time to consider and consult, it also reduces the heat on both sides. But be sure to act on the letter when it does arrive.

If the complaint is serious, warn the management and consult them about how to handle it.

Apart from ringing us directly, listeners have access to three other bodies which can receive and deal with complaints.

- The IBA will write to the station when they receive a complaint and ask for comments or particulars. Under their umbrella, there is also the Independent Complaints Review Board, which can investigate complaints and force a station to correct or amend what was broadcast.
- The Broadcasting Complaints Commission was set up by the Home Office in 1981 to adjudicate on complaints about unjust or unfair treatment in a broadcast, or any unwarranted infringement of privacy while compiling a broadcast. After getting comments from both sides, the Commission will send a copy of their adjudication and a summary of it to the station. Whether or not the complaint is upheld, the Commission will usually direct the station to broadcast its summary at about the same

time as the original programme, but this is the only sanction it has. The Commission does not deal with the depiction of sex or violence, or bad language, or any subject under the broad headings of 'taste' or 'standards'. Those are the province of the Broadcasting Standards Council.

- The Broadcasting Standards Council was created in 1988 with Lord Rees-Mogg as Chairman. It is in the process of drawing up a code of practice on the portrayal of sex and violence, and standards of taste and decency, in radio and television. Its brief includes monitoring programmes in those areas and making findings on complaints about matters within its remit. So far, at least, that remit only covers the areas set out in this paragraph, but that may be extended. Like the Broadcasting Complaints Commission, it has the power to require stations to broadcast its findings following a complaint.

Broadcasters have a duty to inform and stimulate debate in a responsible and objective manner, and within the bounds of good taste. In return we get some flimsy protection from the law, but generally we are on our own. On top of all this, we also have to entertain. Don't be daunted. Putting together good programmes is challenging, but it is also good fun.

4

Writing for Radio

Before you sit down to write a script, consider the components of writing. Words are our stock in trade. We can use sound effects to bring the listener with us part of the way, but in the end it is our words that have to be precise and meaningful. Excellent books have been written on the use of English, but as a general principle, remember Sir Ernest Gowers's advice in *Complete Plain Words*: 'Think for others rather than yourself'. Assess your script before it hits the listener.

Think carefully about the words you choose to use. Words have precise meanings, and if you do decide to misuse them, you should at least be aware of what you are doing. For example, a word that is now commonly misused, especially by politicians, is 'refute' in place of 'deny'. The correct meaning of 'refute' is 'disprove'.

The other demon of the language is the cliché. Despite Sam Goldwyn's advice to 'avoid clichés like the plague', there may be an argument for using a cliché when that is the word the listener will understand without having to think about it. Which words are clichés, or at least over-worked, changes with time, but as a simple exercise, go through the papers, pick out the clichés and decide which word you would have used instead. The tabloids will give you a long list, but the 'qualities' will also provide a fair share.

When we are writing scripts, we try to find different ways to describe what has happened so that we do not sound repetitious, but do be careful not to use words of the wrong weight and tone. If something is 'claimed', is it said, declared, asserted, submitted, contended or maintained? Any one could be correct, but each implies slightly different motives.

Also, think about the construction of words. 'The ship was evacuated' is a fact, but 'The ship had to be evacuated' is a judgment that should be attributed.

Remember the listener

When writing for radio, you should aim to create vivid 'sound pictures' in the listener's mind. The listener has no way of knowing that your face is registering surprise or scepticism, or that you are looking out over a field that should be green but is parched with drought. It is your words that tell the story, so choose them on the basis of their weight, clarity and expressiveness.

Unlike a reader, the listener cannot stop and go back over what has been broadcast. You must therefore use words that are easily understood on first hearing.

You will find your job easier if you remember certain tried and tested guidelines, summarised as follows:

L **Logical**	Your association of ideas should unfold in a logical way, so that the listener doesn't get lost along the way. Signpost changes of direction, e.g. by saying 'So in practice, it may happen like this.'
I **Idiomatic**	Your language should be conversational in tone and style. Write as you speak, rather than according to the the strict rules of grammar and punctuation. You can end sentences with prepositions, and add full stops to incomplete sentences if the result is a natural, conversational style. Use contractions: say 'don't' instead of 'do not' and 'can't' instead of 'cannot', etc.

S **Singular**	You are talking to *one* listener. Don't talk about your 'listeners' or 'audience'. Talk to the single solitary listener as you would to a friend – don't talk down to or at that friend, but get the point *across*.
T **Terse**	Limit your information. Don't overload your script with too much information. Your listener won't be able to take it all in, will lose interest and switch off (either physically or mentally). Try to cut through factual details and go for the whole picture. Avoid statistics, and if you must use numbers, deal in round numbers.
E **Easy**	Your script should be easy to understand and follow. Write in simple, straightforward sentences. As a rule, try to stick to *one* idea per sentence. Use words that anybody will instantly understand.
N **Noteworthy**	Be concrete. Talk in pictures and images to illustrate points. Avoid abstractions.
E **Expanding**	The listener may not be able to absorb an idea right away, so expand on it until it is fully understood before moving on. When you need to repeat a point, find a new way of saying it.
R **Riveting**	Your script should catch and *hold* the listener's attention. Try to involve the listener as much as possible by consciously seeking a response and provoking thought. Build word pictures and illustrate points with analogies. Vary your approach and use different angles.

Telling the story

This section has been written in radio style, so you should

be able to read it out loud and make it conversational.

> Tell 'em you're going to tell 'em.
> Tell 'em.
> Tell 'em you told 'em.

Childlike simplicity is the essence of writing for radio. When people exchange news in the pub or over a cup of tea, they tell it in perfect radio style:

> 'Fred's been taken to hospital ...'
> 'Doreen's husband's left her ...'
> 'That Jones boy is in trouble again ...'

So tell the story as though you're telling it in the pub. Remember that your friends are educated and intelligent, but they may only half hear what you say at the beginning. If you say 'Rates in London are to go up', you'll grab their attention. But if you say 'The Finance Committee of the London Residuary Board reported last night that expenditure forecasts show an increase which may have to be passed on to householders', nobody will know what you're talking about ... and you'll run out of breath before the end of the sentence.

Treat the first sentence as your headline. It must grab the listener's attention and signal that you're saying something interesting.

Even after you've made the first bold statement, remember that the listener may only be half aware of what you said. How often do you have to listen again (where did he say that train crashed?) only to find the newsreader doesn't tell you?

So when you 'tell 'em', your second paragraph should repeat the main point, albeit in disguise: 'The average increase is expected to put fifteen per cent on rate bills.'

So in telling the story, you first *alert* the listener, then *inform*: 'There's a major fire at the Barking chemical works. A hundred homes in the Ilford Lane area near the plant have been evacuated, but firemen say there's little danger of an explosion.'

Get to know as much about every story as you can. You can't write a good script if you don't know the subject, and the listener will always know when you're hedging. But even if you know all the details, don't get too involved in the minutiae of the story. Keep it simple and easy for the listener to follow. If *you* find it difficult to understand, the listener will find it impossible.

Don't overwhelm the listener with unnecessary complexities: 9.65 per cent is 'nearly ten per cent'; 900 yards is 'just over half a mile'; £4,898,247 is 'nearly five million pounds'.

If someone's being quoted in ordinary conversation, people usually start with their title or occupation. This gives an idea of how much importance should be attached to the statement, and also sounds more natural: 'The butcher says the price of lamb's going up,' *not* 'The price of lamb's going up next week, the butcher says.'

Start with the person's *title* or *position*. Don't start with a name unless the person is so well known that the listener will know who it is without having to think about it – and that probably only applies to Margaret Thatcher.

Use the present tense as much as you can. Newspapers have to print yesterday's news. The great advantage of radio is its immediacy, so emphasise it. If you're writing a story about something that happened in the morning for a programme that'll go out in the afternoon, don't use the past tense. Even if this isn't the first opportunity you've had to tell the tale, tell it in the present.

Avoid subordinate clauses. Marshal your facts in short sentences, avoiding commas or brackets.

'The horse, owned and trained by Mrs Mollie Clark and bought last year for fifteen hundred pounds from the Irish trainer, Jim Jones, former owner of the Derby winner Argos, is dead.'

Who's dead? While the listener is trying to work out who's died, he or she might as well be wearing ear-plugs. Anything else you say simply won't be heard.

Be sure you clearly understand the information that

needs to be told. If Tamils are blockading Sri Lanka's ports as part of a major strike, why are you telling me? Is it because tea supplies will soon be running short? If so, tell me, and tell me in the first sentence. In Sri Lanka, the top line would be the strike itself. So far as I'm concerned, it's the morning cuppa that matters.

If you're writing about a foreign country, tell the listener where it is. Geography isn't everyone's strongest subject.

If you find that you're writing yourself into a corner, or that your copy's getting complicated, stop and ask yourself 'What's the point?' Remind yourself why the story is important and which points need to be made. Then get a clean sheet of paper and start again. It's worth doing this even if the deadline is pressing (and in radio, deadlines always seem to be pressing). Otherwise, the copy you send to air will be confusing and a waste of time.

While it's right to use contractions such as 'can't', revert to the full form if you want special emphasis: 'You *cannot* be serious!'

Although you're trying to squeeze as much information as you can into as few words as possible, it's sometimes better on the ear to use a longer form. It's headline journalese to say 'bid' instead of 'attempt', or 'probe' rather than 'investigate' or 'look into'. A 'shares price plunge after conciliation bid fails to win strike pact' may be understandable when you can read it twice, but that's a luxury radio doesn't offer. In any case, have you ever heard anyone in the pub talking that way?

Abbreviations

Very few initials should be used. Those generally recognised by the public are AA, RAC, TUC, NHS, RAF, BBC, IRA and RSPCA.

When you do use initials, identify them and clarify what they mean. For example, ASLEF = the rail union; NUM = the miners' union; NUPE = the public employees' union.

When you can, leave the initials out: 'The miners' union

chief, Arthur Scargill ...', or 'Ken Gill of the white-collar union ...'.

If you do use initials, give the full form first: 'Doctors at the British Medical Association want tougher warnings on cigarette packets. The BMA say the present regulations ...', not 'The BMA say there should be tougher warnings...'.

Cues

There are very few ad libs on radio. Almost every word spoken is scripted in advance. Many presenters even script up the openings: 'Hello, welcome to the programme. I'm Joe Bloggs and today we're going to ...'. It isn't that Joe Bloggs is afraid that he will forget his own name (though I have heard presenters read out their initials instead of their names because that was how it was scripted), it has to do with considerations of flow and timing.

Radio is governed by the clock, and you have to know how long everything will take. There are times when the introduction, or 'cue', to a tape is longer than the actuality itself. While some flexibility can be built in, if you are planning to run a dozen tapes in an hour-long programme, you have to know whether those items will leave the hour light, or whether you should re-edit some of them, or find earlier 'pots', in order fit everything in.

A 'pot' is not a jam-jar. It is a place on the tape where transmission can be stopped, even though the tape has not run its full length. Pots probably got their name from the old days of radio when volume was controlled by potentiometers, or 'pots', and a tape could be ended early by turning the knob quickly to zero during a breath or pause. For practical purposes, though, it could stand for 'pulled off transmission'.

Finding pots on tapes before they go on air gives you flexibility, and means that you can get out of a tape neatly if you are short of time or an important story breaks. Taking 'blind' pots, i.e. trying to second guess where to pot while the tape is going out on air, is usually messy and could be dangerous for legal or contextual reasons.

There are various reasons why some tapes should not be potted, such as that the best bit is at the very end, or in the interests of balance. In such cases a note that the tape is not pottable should go onto the cue.

The cue must fulfil the following functions:

- Alert the listener to the new item.
- Introduce the report or actuality.
- Give extra information or up-dates not carried in the report or actuality, perhaps from other sources or stories.
- Link the material with a preceding item if necessary.

A good cue will also act as 'insurance', giving the listener sufficient information to understand the story should the audio fail to materialise for some reason. But it should not give away the punch line.

The cue also carries operating information vital to the presenter, engineer and producer:

- The catchline, or 'slug', which identifies the story.
- The date and time of writing.
- The author's name, and an indication of other sources used.
- The duration of the audio.
- The outcue of the audio.
- The duration and outcues of pots.
- The total duration of cue and audio combined. Some computers which have been specially programmed for use in broadcasting can calculate the total running time of both script and audio, but if you need to work out the duration of a cue manually, count three words as one second.
- In the case of a news cut, the story number, and
- The cut number.

A typical cue embracing all these programme requirements might look like this:

Lebanon wrap/Addicott 1730 update PA/UPI 21 June

There's a new attempt by President Bush to obtain the release of the American hostages in Beirut.

The President's sent a personal letter to his Lebanese counterpart calling for their release on humanitarian grounds.

In London, American students are picketing the Lebanese Embassy, and there have been two arrests. But our reporter, Bill Addicott, says the picketing is mainly peaceful.
TAPE:
DUR: 2:53
OUT Q: ...UNTIL THE MORNING.
TOTAL 3:14
POT Q: ...AT ABOUT MIDNIGHT.
POT DUR: 1:32

This cue tells us that the story is about Lebanon, and that it is a wrap (see p. 94) written by Bill Addicott at 5.30 pm. It is updated, which means it supersedes any other tapes on Lebanon, and material from the wire services PA and UPI was used in it. The date should be the date the tape is to be transmitted: if you do not include it, an archivist somewhere will curse you. The tape runs for 2 minutes 53 seconds, and the cue and tape together will take 3 minutes 14 seconds, unless it is potted at 1 minute 32 seconds.

Never finish a cue with the same words as appear at the beginning of the tape – it jars and sounds silly. For example, do not finish your cue with 'He told me he was exhausted' when the tape begins 'I'm exhausted'. Find another formulation, such as 'He told me the experience was a test of his endurance.'

Your voice

You will have to find your own pace and style in front of the mike. Experiment with your voice – you will be surprised what you can do by varying your intonation and speed of delivery. There is no substitute for practice, but a few hints may speed the process up.

First of all, you are not talking into a microphone. You are talking to a friend who is sitting no more than six feet from you. Do not shout. Learn to convey urgency and authority by varying your pace and tone.

The listener should never be aware that you are reading from a script. 'Reading conversationally' (and without rattling the paper) comes naturally to some people, but most of us have to practise to get it right. Picturing your friend helps, because the apparatus and the thought that strangers are listening can be off-putting. So forget the mike, and just tell the story.

You must understand what you're reading. If you do not, you will not be able to give the story the correct stress and inflection. For example, read out the phrase 'What's the matter with you?' putting the emphasis on different words each time. The different stresses alter the meaning. Most presenters and reporters mark their scripts, underlining key words that need to be stressed and putting in back slashes or asterisks to show where they should take a breath or pause.

Quotation marks should not often appear in radio scripts. But when they do, you indicate their presence by a small pause both times and a very slight change of tone: 'Mr Kinnock says the measures are // "too restrictive" // and thinks they should be withdrawn.'

Your delivery should be measured, no matter how fast or slow you go. The average speaking pace is three words per second. Some people naturally speak faster or slower than this, and you will have to see what your 'norm' is.

You should aim to speak fast enough to maintain interest, but slow enough to keep the listener with you.

Your voice must convey credibility. Be sure to project well; do not mumble, but equally do not bombard the poor listener or get so close to the mike that you pop. 'Popping' is an exploding noise that happens when a 'p' or 'b' gets thrown at the microphone so hard that it cannot cope.

Going back to the pub for a minute, as we sit and talk we communicate thoughts, and we think (and listen) in groups of words and phrases. Learn to read your script in the same way. This will depend somewhat on having a well-written script in the first place. If it's written conversationally, it can be read conversationally.

Your voice will also convey your facial expression. Just

try to sound serious while reading with a smile on your face.

Read scripts aloud before you record them or go to air, so you know when a sentence or phrase is more than one breath's worth. Mark where you are going to take the extra breath.

Figures should always be written out. It is difficult to interpret a series of noughts on air, and if there is a typographical error in a written word, it will be less disastrous than if a figure is wrong. So write 'more than a million' rather than 'more than 1,000,000' and 'a hundred and thirty have died', not '130 have died'. If the script actually reads 'a hundred and thorty have died', the chances are that it will come out right on air, but if it reads '140 have died', there's no hope. And, although this is not the main consideration, writing figures out also keeps your word count accurate.

Just one additional word of caution about figures. In sports stories, does '0' mean nought, love, zero, oh, or nil? The listener knows, so if you don't, find out. A presenter at City in Liverpool once managed to light up the station switchboard when she reported that Liverpool football club had beaten a German team by 'four goals to love'.

You can speak loudly without shouting if you use projection. This is a skill that actors and singers learn, and so should you. Project your voice from your diaphragm, not from your vocal chords. To find out where your diaphragm is, you should first of all be sure you're in a room on your own so people won't think you've gone a bit peculiar, then pant like a dog. Keep panting for a couple of minutes (but be careful not to hyperventilate), and that horizontal band near your waist that begins to ache is it. Your diaphragm is a muscle, and like all muscles it gets stronger with use and exercise.

You can add authority to your delivery by lowering the register of your voice, which is especially useful for some female voices. Articulate the words of the script clearly, and pounce on them rather than allowing the words to trickle out. Remember that the end of the sentence is as important as the beginning, so do not let your voice trail off.

The most important thing is to know what you are talking about. It is credibility you are after, and that comes with knowledge, understanding and authority.

5

Getting the Story

Commercial radio's approach to stories tends to be punchier than the BBC's, and more colloquial language is used. Our delivery is very different, our pace is usually faster, and our aim is to 'bring the story home' to the listener.

There are times when even the choice of story will be different. The BBC tends to carry more foreign stories, while we will often leave them until they harden up. For example, the BBC was running the Japanese Prime Minister's efforts to resist resignation more often, although everyone pounced on the story when the announcement came that he was going to resign.

For all the differences between the services, if you put the editors together in a room their overall approach would not be very different. There is fierce competition to get a story to air first. If a big story breaks, everyone goes for the best, fastest and most thorough coverage. Since commercial radio is smaller and leaner, we do not have so many tiers to get through. This sometimes means we can scramble faster.

The resources available to the BBC and IRN are very different. When the Kuwaiti Airlines 747 was hijacked and the story needed coverage from three foreign capitals, IRN's resources were stretched almost to breaking point. It is a credit to the energy and resourcefulness of those who work in the system that the listener cannot tell that commercial radio is operating with a fraction of the BBC's resources.

News sources

The most important source of news is your involvement in the community, knowing what is affecting it and what people care about. That involvement is vital if your news judgment is to be sound, but it is also your most basic source of information, whether national or local.

Journalists build up individual contacts over the years who become valuable sources of news. These are people who come to know and trust a particular journalist and will ring when something of interest or importance is happening. But individual contacts are the thoroughbreds in the stable. The workhorses form part of the day-to-day organisation of the newsroom itself.

The first general guide you turn to on any particular day is the 'news diary' – a compilation of all the news releases received by the station concerning events for that day. The hard news releases are separated from the 'what's on' variety, the former being of interest to the news desk, the latter possibly for use on air as a public service. Given that all newsrooms are flooded with news releases (stations in large cities can get hundreds in one day), you might think that they would generate a large number of stories. Alas, we do our duty and sift through them all, but well over 90 per cent of them meet their Waterloo with little more than a glance. Wastepaper bins in newsrooms tend towards the commodious variety.

The diary will also contain reminders of events or updates for running stories, such as the starting date for an inquiry, the resumption of a court case, or the day a group of charity walkers are expected to return. The date is circled, with the notation 'D & F', which stands for Diary and File.

Fax machines have certainly come into their own – so much so that I have heard colleagues pleading with people *not* to fax something but post it instead. Faxes should really be used only for urgent information that stands some chance of staying out of the wastepaper bin. In any case, fax copies are usually more difficult to read than the original.

The Press Association publishes a daily general prospects list, showing the major stories they will be covering on that day. It sometimes runs on the wire for the first time at about 04.30 and is then repeated later, or it may come across just once at about 08.30.

IRN also compiles a prospects list each morning in order to let all the stations in the network know which stories the editor intends to cover. An updated prospects list goes out mid-afternoon giving evening and overnight stories that will be covered.

Once those basic sources have been checked, it is a matter of check calls, tip-offs (see pp. 80-1) and keeping an eye on the wires.

News wires

News wires are information services hired out to clients. The programme desks and IRN have three general news wires available, plus the UNS service. The news wires are the Press Association (PA), Reuters, and United Press International (UPI). Teletext TVs in the newsrooms enable you to keep a check on Ceefax and Oracle, but their coverage tends to be brief – more like a headline than a full story – and the length of time it takes them to process stories often means we have already had the story to air before it appears on the screen.

The wires are used constantly, but for different things depending on the story and which job is being done. They may sometimes be used as a basis for voicing up a story before a reporter can get to the scene or before we can get actuality, but we also rely on our own sources, not only because it is good journalistic practice, but also because we need to be completely on top of stories immediately. The wires are designed for newspapers, so they may be slower than we can accept, and they are geared to deadlines that are anathema to us.

New stories can appear on the Newstar computer at a rate of about fifty in ten minutes, so the wires are obviously feeding us a lot of information which needs to be sifted. On the newsdesk this is done by the 'copy taster', who keeps a check on everything running on all the wires and alerts the editor to a new story or angle if necessary. In programme terms, producers and reporters scan the wires and use the information according to their needs.

Press Association (PA)

The Press Association's general slug on the computer is pah (pa highwire). It has a staff of about 250 journalists and deals with domestic stories in the main, covering foreign stories only when they have a domestic connection. When an IRA bomb went off in Germany, for instance, PA's defence team carried details of what was happening in Germany because there were obvious connections with the Ministry of Defence here. In the case of a ferry that was sprayed with gunfire in Greece, however, PA picked up the story when the schoolgirls who had been on the boat got back to Heathrow.

Once a story has opened on PA, it continues to use the same slug for each subsequent up-date or rewrite. For instance, during the Richmond by-election, every story dealing with the campaign was slugged 'Richmond'.

PA gives you the story in short spurts or 'takes', and each take is numbered. In the case of the IRA bomb blast in Germany, the number of takes went into double figures for several days. Each day's coverage starts with take number 1, and there are times when the takes do not even appear in chronological order. PA is used in the newsroom as a back-up service for details of stories or background. It is also a source for breaking stories, but we very often get notice of a story from our own sources before it appears on PA.

Sometimes PA runs a 'snap' – a very brief indication that something important has happened, which is often not even in complete sentence form. In due course, it will put out a 'snapful' (a fuller write-through of the story), but this may take some time, which is another reason why we rely on our own sources.

Takes, snaps and snapfuls have been mentioned. Other terms you will come across include:

- Lead: a new write-through that may include new information.
- Substitute: a re-write of a story after a correction or after new information.
- Background: information which complements a running story. It does not necessarily give any details about the actual story that prompted the backgrounder.
- List: the day's diary of main stories and how PA will cover them.
- Advisory: a message telling you what to expect from PA and when if it differs from the list.
- Overnight re-write: what it says. A condensed version of the story which does not introduce any new material.

Reuters

Reuters is an international news service, but we use it mainly as a source of foreign news. Reuters became a public company in 1984, and London is just one of its main bases, albeit the original one. Its computer slug is rtu. Like PA, Reuters gives you the story in spurts, but its takes are usually a bit longer. It employs about 1200 journalists in 80 countries and 181 cities, and that number is topped up by the use of 'stringers', or freelancers. Their terminology includes:

- Scheduled: an expected story which they had advised they would be covering.
- 1stld: 'first lead', a re-write which may include new information.
- Urgent: a major story that is just breaking.

United Press International (UPI)

UPI is an American wire (its main US rival is AP, or Associated Press). It does not run as many stories as PA and Reuters, and they are obviously written from an American point of view (including angles, timings for filing, writing style and spelling). UPI is a useful back-up or alternative to Reuters because most of its stories are foreign. If it does cover a domestic story, it is not usually as comprehensive as PA or our own sources.

Universal News Services (UNS)

This is a service which news-makers can use. Clients (often companies or unions) pay UNS to put out full statements or press releases on their wire. A UNS journalist can write the story for them in journalese, or clients can hire the UNS audio service to send a recorded Q & A to radio stations. While the copy taster keeps a watch on everything UNS puts through, the service is not used a lot by either newsdesks or programmes (except the city desk) because the subject matter is either too particular for us or, if they are running statements on stories we are covering, those statements will have come through directly to the newsroom.

Specialist wires

Two departments in IRN are supplied with their own specialist wires: sport and city.

Sport has 5 wires: Xtel general, which is a special sports service; greyhounds; racing (of the horse variety); PA and Reuters, both of whom send only sport stories on this wire.

City's specialist service is made up of mainly Reuters and UNS, with an occasional story from PA. All the stories are city or business based. City also uses Telerate, a direct service from the financial markets for exchange rates, and Datastream, a computer system which gives up-to-date stock-market prices.

Independent Radio News (IRN)

IRN has staff correspondents and stringers in most major

cities, but almost all staff are based in the London newsroom. The journalists who cover Parliament are based at Bridge Street, just across the road from Westminster Palace. IRN provides the network stations, which number about 50, with national and international news. Stations can opt into the on-hour news live from the London studios, or compile bulletins locally from all the components that are regularly fed to them on circuits (including cues, cuts and snaps). IRN also supplies the network with headlines for half-hourly news summaries, and each hour a 'billboard' service of programme-length tapes is fed out.

The role of the copy taster has already been mentioned, but here are the other IRN positions.

* The *reader/writer* reads each bulletin from IRN's London studio and is also responsible for writing and sending to the network summaries of the three or four main stories which will be read out at approximately half-past each hour. These headlines are usually no longer than one or two sentences, but must give the latest and most important angles of each story. The reader/writer will also help to prepare items for the bulletins that go out on the hour.

* The *bulletin editor* decides which stories will go into each bulletin, and in what order, prepares the items and makes sure that the newsreader gets the right amount of material to fill the bulletin. Bulletins range from two to four minutes.

* The *duty editor* has overall responsibility for IRN's coverage during the course of a shift, and also participates in the preparation of each bulletin. The duty editor takes the final decisions on which stories and which angles will be run.

* The *intake editor* liaises with the duty editor, and is responsible for organising coverage and getting stories in-house. Depending on the story, that may mean contacting a local station and asking reporters there to cover it, briefing a freelance, sending an IRN reporter, or getting a reporter to voice up what has happened.

IRN reporters work in a staggered shift system, so that there are reporters available 24 hours a day.

Reference books

Some reference books are particularly useful. You should make yourself familiar with at least those listed here.

- *Who's Who* lists people in this country who the editors have decided are important. The entries are in alphabetical order and are based on information supplied by the entrants themselves. Each entry gives a summary of the person's career and interests, as well as who they are married to, how many children they have, etc. It also gives some kind of contact point (a club or sometimes a home address and phone number).
- *International Who's Who* covers people who are well known internationally, and is compiled on the same basis as *Who's Who*.
- *Dod's Parliamentary Companion* lists all the current members of Parliament sitting in both the Commons and the Lords. It will tell you when they entered Parliament, what posts they hold or have held, and which issues they are particularly interested in. There are other good Parliamentary guides, but *Dod's* is among those with a reputation for accuracy.
- *Directory of British Associations* is a gem. It lists almost every association in the country which is not a government body or quango, giving details of the purpose of the organisation, who is in charge and the address and phone number. It includes everybody from AAA (Action Against Allergy) to the Zip Manufacturers Association (with apologies to the Zoological Societies of Glasgow and London).
- *British Books in Print* lists every book currently in print in the UK. It is cross-referenced according to subject, title and author. It can be a starting point for finding an expert in a particular field, but you will not be able to tell what any author's prejudice may be.

online?

- *Willing's Press Guide* lists all the newspapers and journals registered in Britain. It can help you find a contact in a specialised field: the British seem to support magazines or papers on almost any specialised subject you can think of, and the editor probably keeps up to date.
- *Statesman's Year Book* can make you an instant expert on any country with which Britain has diplomatic relations. It gives a short history of each country, a summary of the economy, something about the major cities and some geography, as well as listing the names of the diplomatic personnel and the telephone number of the British embassy or mission.
- *Guinness Book of Records*. The index at the back will direct you to your subject.
- *Screen International Film and TV Yearbook* lists actors, producers, directors, etc., and all the films or programmes they have been involved in.
- *International Film Encyclopedia* (ed. Katz). All the entries are based on people, events, etc. in film, e.g. the 'Italy' entry gives that country's history in the film industry.
- *Halliwell's Film Guide* covers more than 15,000 films and tells you what each film was about, who wrote it, starred in it and sometimes what the critics said about it. You may not agree with Leslie Halliwell's opinions, but he will tell you just about anything you need to know about a film.
- *Oxford Companion to the Theatre*. Like the film encyclopedia, lists people, events, etc. based on the theatre.
- *Music Master* and *MM Track Index*. *Music Master* lists international singers or groups alphabetically and all the albums or singles they have recorded. The *Track Index* is an alphabetical list of song titles and who recorded them.
- *Guinness British Hit Singles* is split into three sections. The first two are alphabetical listings of artists and titles. The third part lists 'Facts and Feats', including 'Most Weeks in Chart' and 'Least Successful Chart Act'.
- *Oxford Dictionary of Quotations*. Lists well-known quotations. Useful if you want to quote accurately, check who

said it, or find an appropriate quotation. If, for instance, you want a quote with the word 'write' in it, you will be directed to Shakespeare's 'have to write me down ar. ass'. You would find the same quote under 'ass'.
- *Whitaker's Almanac*, which you must already know.

Most newsrooms keep a library of newspaper cuttings, which are a good source of recent stories and profiles of the famous. Always photocopy the cuttings you want to use and return the originals. Similarly, if a tape archive section is kept, dub off any interview or the part of it that you want to use and replace the tape in its box in its full form. *Never cut any part of an archive tape!*

Reporting

Getting that exclusive interview or digging up a story that causes a crisis in government is every reporter's dream, but even the most experienced investigative reporter does not stumble over such gems every day, and no sensational story is ever a gift. Hard work, determination and attention to detail lie behind every big story. We all learn to take short-cuts, but it is important to be aware of the dangers of taking them. So learn the craft well and build up a good solid background.

A good reporter will always find out from the editor or producer what angle is required, how long the piece should run, and when it is needed. These three items of information *must* be the first you ascertain. They may be obvious, but if ever you are not sure, it doesn't matter how busy the editor or producer is, find out. Otherwise you will almost certainly waste time chasing the wrong angle.

The other essential quality of any good reporter is knowing that anything *can* be a story and being keen to get it. A good reporter will do as good a job putting together a piece about a siege as one about the awarding of the title 'Loo of the Year'.

There was once an editor at IRN who had a gift for convincing reporters that if they 'did this one right' it could lead the bulletin. The wonderful thing was, even duff stories often ended up being well placed! Install a bit of that editor in your mind. Aim to make every piece you do worthy of being the lead.

Contacts

Every journalist needs a good contacts book containing every possible useful number. A contacts book is almost always the first stage of getting to a story, and being able to get to the right person fast is all-important. Take photocopies of each page of your contacts book regularly so that if it is lost you are not left wanting your right arm.

If you have a memory like a sieve, work out a way of cross-indexing your book so that you can find numbers quickly. One system is to divide each letter of the alphabet into three sections: people, organisations and subjects. Then, if a story breaks in India, for example, you can turn to the subjects section under 'I' and find a list of people and organisations with expert knowledge of India. If you use a loose-leaf binder, it will be easier to add pages to sections that become full, or replace pages that become largely redundant. There are personal pocket computers available which can store all the information for you, but be sure you have a hard copy of it somewhere.

News releases and embargos

If you are doing a story from a news release, your job will be made that little bit easier. The release will not only sell you the story (without necessarily telling you the whole tale), it will also give you contact names and numbers.

The contacts are normally PRs, who are almost *never* the right people to talk to on tape. They are not decision-makers but information disseminators. They are therefore most unlikely to be able to answer questions such as 'What are you going to do about it?' Go for the person at the top.

Try not to waste time by letting people say they will ring you back. Tell them you will hold on. This demonstrates that you are serious, and that you think they are important. Moreover phones have a compulsive quality – how many people do you know who ignore a ringing telephone just because they are involved in an important conversation?

If you are trying to get someone to come in to the studio, or if the person you want to talk to is not around or difficult to get to, then you may have to wait for a call back. Just be aware that you are putting yourself in *their* hands rather than being in control yourself.

The news release may carry an 'embargo', which is a request to hold publication of the information until a particular date and time. An embargo is sometimes included for practical and sensible reasons, such as when it is timed to a particular event or the publication of a report. At other times it is difficult to see the sense of an embargo, and it may be that the organisers are trying to manipulate the timing for their own reasons. For example, it is well-known within the industry that Mondays are 'bad news' days because fewer newsworthy events tend to happen on Sunday. Therefore items that would probably not get a look-in most other days just might 'make' on a Monday.

Embargos carry no statutory weight, although there might be a case for a breach of copyright claim in some circumstances. So far as I know, however, no one has brought such a case. When an embargo is broken the more usual remedy is an internal one within the industry, such as withdrawing facilities.

For example, the Queen's Honours List always comes out in advance under a 'strict embargo' so that we can organise pre-recorded interviews with people on the list and have coverage ready as soon as the embargo comes off. Until 1987 no one ever broke the embargo. Then the *Sun* ran a story on two Zeebrugge heroes who were to receive the George Medal the day before the New Year Honours list came off embargo. Since then the Palace has released the names just twelve hours before the embargo rather than giving the two days' advance notice we used to get.

Government department embargos are seldom broken, but since politicians can be nearly as cynical as journalists, big announcements are often preceded only by a terse invitation to a news conference, just in case. If you are faced with such an invitation, it is worth ringing the department's press office. They will sometimes tell you over the phone what they are not willing to put on paper; at the very least, you should be able to find out whether it is going to be an important announcement that needs to be covered.

If you want to break an embargo, you will usually have to get the originator's agreement in order to get any actuality. That is one of the drawbacks of radio. If a newspaper breaks an embargo, on the other hand, broadcasters must either chase the story at double speed or ditch it; if it is in the papers the listener may think we are a day behind. If the story is still worth telling, at least any resistance will have been broken down by the paper's report.

Sourcing

One of the rules of reporting is that every story should be 'double sourced'. If a dependable reporter has not seen or heard something first hand, get confirmation of the facts from another source before running it. This may be difficult, but it is one of the times when you must employ the 'if in doubt, leave it out' rule. A good story may be knocking about, but if you cannot harden it up it is dangerous to run it.

If the first you hear of a story is when it comes up on the wires, still check it. Our colleagues in all the major services are first-rate, but even the best of us can make mistakes, and the story may have moved on since the reporter filed the copy. But, more important, this is radio. Copy filed on the wires will at least have to be rewritten before it is voiced up, but we need more. We need actuality and colour!

Tip-offs

Tip-offs can be useful, whether from freelances (whom you

have to pay) or from listeners (who are not as reliable). In either case, check the information before you go to air with it. There is a man named Rocky Ryan who has turned hoaxing news organisations into a campaign, and he has been able to plant bogus stories into national outlets. Ryan is well known, but he is still trying – and he may not be the only one.

If you get a tip-off from a listener, thank the person politely but treat the information warily. You are there to get the facts right; moreover what the listener thinks is news may not fit in with the newsroom's definition. Having said that, if it is important to one person, it may be worth checking to see if it has wider appeal. If it is a major local story that you are not on top of, hop to it. You are already late off the mark!

Check calls

One of the most important ways of staying on top of 'your patch' is to contact the emergency services regularly. These are known as *check calls*, and reporters should be in touch with fire, ambulance and police every couple of hours. That is the theory, but like everything else in life the practice may be more complicated.

In larger cities, the emergency services' press rooms often have a taped version of what is happening which press officers will update on a more or less regular basis. Depending on what sort of day it is, or who the press officer is, the tape may be updated less frequently than we would like. The person designated to deal with check calls is not at the scene and may not know the story, let alone the latest. Trying to go directly to the person dealing with an incident as it is happening could make you very unpopular, and ancillary staff may not know what is going on. Be guided by press officers or their subordinates, but remember that there is no substitute for getting to the scene.

At the scene

Once you are there, find out who is in charge and whether anyone else has been designated to keep you informed. Position yourself so that you can see the event (without putting yourself at any risk; a hospitalised reporter is of little use to the newsdesk), and *keep your recorder running*, doing commentaries from the scene regularly to update the desk and for possible use later in a wrap. There is almost nothing more frustrating than to be on the scene and miss the actuality of an explosion, gun fire or angry exchange because you were 'resting' your recorder.

Do not get in the way of the emergency services, but do not be a lamb either. There are situations in which the police will keep you out of the line of sight, e.g. at major sieges where firearms are involved, but they happen very rarely.

Door-stepping

'Door-stepping' is the bane of reporters, but essential to getting certain sorts of stories. There you are in the pouring rain, sitting outside the area that is meant to produce your story; the newsdesk keeps nagging you for an update even though nothing has moved; there is nowhere to get a snack for lunch, let alone a toilet; and you and all the other journos are getting very fed up. Fight boredom. When the story breaks, you will have to respond quickly; if you have become lethargic your poor reaction time may cost you that moment of perfect actuality.

Think about your positioning. For instance, if trade union leaders are meeting with management in an effort to avoid strike action, you should work out where they will probably emerge and position yourself to beat the pack. Newspaper journalists often carry little tape recorders in order to ensure they get the quote right, but they do not have to have broadcast quality. Get your microphone in front of the person who matters – somehow. If you are tall you may be able to reach over other people's shoulders, or if you are small, under their armpits. You may just have to imagine you are on the Tokyo tube and squeeze yourself into a non-existent space. Get there. What is the point of undergoing all those tedious hours just to go back to the desk to tell them your actuality is not broadcastable?

News conferences

The other situation in which you must get your mike in the right place is the news conference. Don't forget the mike stand. If more than one person is making a statement, don't be shy about getting to the table and moving your mike. News conferences are also called *press* conferences, and while we in radio prefer the word news (we don't like being left out), these conferences are designed for print journalists. Supplementary questions from the pack will be off-mike and unusable, which means you will have to wrap it.

Sometimes the actuality from the conference is all you need, or all you can get, but it is usually better to arrange in advance to get your own interview or 'Q & A' afterwards. Press the PR or whoever is making arrangements to let you nip in *before* the TV people. Their equipment takes time to rig up and their interviews take longer to do. They also have to shoot 'cut-aways' or 'noddies' in order to disguise a film edit. By the time they have finished you will probably have missed at least one bulletin, and if there is more than one TV crew around, you will be cooling your heels for quite a while. PRs like getting their story on TV and usually consider it more important than radio, so use the immediacy of radio to get your place in front. 'My editor really wants this story for the next bulletin' flatters them.

Government ministers and some other high-ranking people ask for an advance list of the questions you will ask in the interview. Keep to *areas* rather than specific questions, and remember the phrase 'plus supplementaries'. Without that phrase, some interviewees can get rather prickly about answering anything but the exact subject areas you said you were going to cover, so if they drop a bombshell in one of their answers, they will stall answering your pick-up questions (or even downright refuse).

Sometimes interviewees ask for an advance list when it is not really justified. Tell them politely that it is just a straightforward interview covering the general issues. Giving an advance list not only restricts you, it is also time-consuming, and a radio reporter should always be aware of the clock's relentless second-hand.

Pressure groups

These are another major source of news. They range from the 'worthies' to political and trade unions, and they all have an axe to grind. Often you will find it of interest to your listener to help them at the grindstone, but do not let a bit of panic about filling your air-time influence your decision. You should be able to take a more creative approach, like finding that extra angle on a good story.

Silly seasons

All this may sound as though there are always stories just waiting to be tackled. If only that were true. Of course there are days when good stories stream in and you have to deal with two or three at once. You end up working overtime and go home exhausted but satisfied.

But there is also the silly season. This phrase used to be reserved for the summer (mainly August), but now it is often used to cover any of those times when the only things moving are departing holiday-makers. Parliament, local councils and the courts are major sources of news, and they all take breaks not only in the summer, but also around Christmas and Easter. At such times, even if there is a breaking story, there may well be nobody around to talk about it. This is when a good contacts book and your local knowlege become your life-lines.

Working away from base

Every reporter wants to cover the big story, but if that story is a hijack in Athens, you haven't a hope of being sent unless you have your passport. Every other piece of equipment you need can be taken from the newsroom or purchased later. Get in the habit of having your passport on you at all times.

Working away from base is a testing time. You will need to call on all your resourcefulness and reserves of energy. You will have to find someone who speaks English for actuality, or at least for translation (unless you speak Greek). Hourly bulletins and regular programmes demand constant updating, so if you are working for a station that is on air twenty-four hours a day it may be difficult to get any sleep.

The IRN reporter first sent to cover the Zeebrugge disaster got something like four hours' sleep in the first 48 she was there, and it was into the third day before she had time to buy a change of clothes. That is not unusual, but the problems encountered by the reporter covering the Algerian leg of the Kuwaiti Airlines hijack were unique.

All the journalists covering the story were staying in the hotel near the airport when the authorities suddenly told them that they would all have to leave. The newspaper reporters grumbled, but they could move into hotels in the city centre. No such luck for the broadcast journalists who had to meet hourly deadlines.

With a bit of unofficial prodding, the radio journalists got a phone line stretched out into a field that had line of sight to the plane. John Cookson fed his reports down the line which was tacked to a pole stuck in the middle of the field. He had to interrupt his reports occasionally to stop chickens pecking at his legs.

Eventually a survival kit arrived from the newsdesk, containing a tent, a sleeping bag and some packaged instant food. Ramadan was about to begin, so he would not be able to get any food during daylight hours. Perhaps if they had thought of sending along some chicken feed, the hens would have left his legs alone.

Luckily the hijack ended a few days later, so he didn't have to endure these conditions too long, but it was an extreme example of the loneliness of the long-distance reporter.

Interviewing

Interviews on radio carry a stronger impact than those in the press, because the listener often deduces as much information from *how* a question is answered as from the actual words spoken. If the interviewee hesitates before answering, that pause may tell the listener at least as much as the words that eventually follow.

Your job is to get the interviewee to divulge facts, reasons or opinions. Do not forget the basic rule that your opinions simply do not matter. You need to do your homework before the interview and listen carefully while it is going on, but your opinions must not get in the way.

The first kind of interview a story is likely to require is the straightforward *informative* sort. When a story first breaks, you need to find out exactly what has happened. You may be just as much in the dark as the listener, and your questions will flow from a natural inquisitiveness or from the interviewee's replies. If, for example, there has been a major fire at a chemical plant, the senior fire officer may be interviewed about how it started, whether there is a danger to residents in the area, etc. But if, during the course of the interview, it emerges that this particular plant has had a series of fires, the interview may change direction.

At that point, the fire officer may be asked *interpretative* questions, such as whether fire safety regulations had been observed or whether they are good enough. Interpretative interviews are trying to get behind the facts so that the listener can put the issue into perspective. It could be anything from asking the Chancellor why interest rates had to go up to why a particular performance by a ballet company did not come up to scratch.

The most difficult kind of interview to do is the *emotional*. If there has been an explosion at a mine, with miners trapped underground, it is an intrusion to ask wives and families gathered at the pit head how they feel. It is not just an intrusion on them, it also intrudes on the listener. Emotional interviews convey the human side of a story, and sharing an experience is an important part of life that has its place. You must, though, put yourself in the place of the interviewee. 'When did you first hear about the accident' is a more appropriate question. The stress and worry will come through. Or at the other end of the scale, the delight and relief will come across once all the men are found safe. It is when the emotion is pleasurable that it is appropriate to ask 'How do you feel'.

The *personality* interview, on the other hand, is meant to be entertaining and revealing. It usually involves a celebrity, but can extend to anyone well-known, from politicians to union leaders. The basis of the interview is always the person rather than an event. Be sensitive when the interview strays into emotional areas. The interviewee may start talking about how drugs or drink was a problem at some time, or the effect of the death of someone close. It is an important part of that person's life, and therefore belongs in the interview, but find a way of bringing the interview back to positive aspects in order to end on a high note.

If you are going for this sort of interview, be sure that the interviewee knows what you want. Some people in the public eye resent probing questions about their private lives.

The IBA lays down these four basic guidelines for all interviews:

- If a person is interviewed as a representative of an organisation or group, you *must* be sure that the person is entitled to speak on their behalf.
- The interviewee *must* be told how the interview will be used.
- The interviewee *must* be told the identity and role of any other participants in the wrap or programme.
- If the interview takes place over the phone, you *must* be

sure that the interviewee knows it is being taped for possible transmission.

Remember that you are asking the questions on behalf of the listener. You have access to more information, so you may ask questions the listener would not have thought of, but in the end you need to get across the information the listener not only wants to know, but should know.

An interview must be spontaneous, so discuss the general areas that will be covered beforehand without revealing the actual questions. Interviewees will start contriving their answers if they know the actual questions, or, worse, decide to make notes on what they want to say. The result will be a stilted interview that might as well appear in a newspaper.

If you are turned down for an interview, be careful of using the 'No comment' phrase. It can imply that there is something to hide. If someone does not want to react to a report until there has been time to read it, or management does not want to respond to union allegations until there has been a meeting, say so. If the phrase was 'There's no comment at this time', are you giving the listener an accurate reflection if you leave off the last three words? If the answer to that is yes, then go ahead, but consider it first.

When preparing for an interview, you must be clear why you are doing it and what you expect to come out of it. The first half of that equation is usually easier than the second. Do as much research as you can or have time for, because if the interviewee comes up with something startling and you do not understand the background well enough to recognise it, the listener will quite rightly be annoyed.

Some of that research may well involve going back over newspaper clippings. Use the information you find there, but always check it. It may have been wrong in the first place; even if it was accurate, things may have changed since then. For example, in the early days of CND, Bruce Kent did not participate in the Aldermaston marches because he did not believe that was the best way to get the message across; an opinion he no longer holds.

All this assumes you have any time at all. If it is a breaking story, you will have to emulate the emergency services. Get to the scene fast and hope that the information you carry in your head will be good enough in the first instance. That means staying on top of the news and knowing which angles or issues are contentious. If a plane crashes, you need to know whether that particular type of aircraft has been involved in a string of crashes without spending valuable time having to look it up. Most editors expect reporters to have read at least one serious and one popular newspaper each day, and to have seen at least one of the major television news broadcasts.

Before you start any interview, ascertain the basic facts. You must get names, positions and dates right. The interviewee will be irriated if you get them wrong, and if you are constantly having to be corrected over minor matters the main thrust of the interview will be lost.

Talk to the interviewee beforehand to find out what sort of talker he or she is and clarify any facts that you are not sure about. You may also need to calm down nervous people or encourage timid ones. Be straight with people, but do not reveal your punchlines if it is not an informational interview. You can tell someone what areas you plan to cover without giving away your line of attack.

If the interview is to be live, telling the guest the gist of the first question may start it off more smoothly. If it is a pre-recorded interview, the first question should really end up as part of the cue material, or may be designed to put the interviewee at ease – in either case expect the first question and answer to be cut. It can, however, be a useful double-check on levels. People often speak at a different level when they know the machine is recording.

A good interview will cover the '6 W's':

- Who
- What
- Where
- When
- How
- Why

The only one that does not ask for a fact or an interpretation of a fact is 'Why', which asks for an opinion or reason and usually provokes the most interesting response. By the time you have finished your report, all six questions should have been answered either in the interview itself or in a combination of cue and interview.

Avoid questions that start with 'will, 'is', 'did' or 'have' unless you want a single-word answer. You may want to provoke a yes/no reply to vary the pace of the interview or emphasise a particular point. Just know the danger of what you are doing, and be ready with the follow-up question.

Your questions should be clear and simple. Use as few words as you can, and include just one concept per question. Do not make statements unless they are carefully couched; there is a danger of them pulling you out of the objective role. Put the other side of the argument, but do not let it sound like your opinion. Attribute the other side if you can ('The leader of the opposition says the Council is over-spent'); even if it is a general point, distance yourself from it ('Some people may say that the Council is over-spent').

Your questions should progress in a logical way. If you are going to change direction, sign-post the change: 'On a different issue altogether, Councillor, you've been quoted as saying …'

Questions should be neither too broad ('What did you find in your six-month study tour?') nor too narrow ('And how long did little Alice cry after she fell over?').

Never ask leading questions. By definition, they take you out of your objective role. Remember that you are getting the facts, information or opinions of others so that listeners can formulate their own conclusions.

For the same reason, avoid adjectives and adverbs. It is up to the listener to decide whether a 50 per cent increase is large.

Mind your manners. A 'hard' interview is not necessarily aggressive. There are times when an interview becomes adversarial, but the listener should be able to follow why it has done so. You will generally get more out of an interview if you use polite but dogged persistence.

On the other side of the coin, a lot of inexperienced reporters find it difficult to pluck up the courage to ask any questions, even easy ones. It is unnatural to ask prying questions of a perfect stranger, so it is not surprising that many beginners worry about how they are going to perform. Find a formula for settling your nerves. You must always respect the position of the interviewee, but remember that the interview would not be happening if there had not been an agreement for it to take place.

If you want to include a 'tough' question, do not put it first or leave it till last. Put it in about third or fourth – by then the interviewee's guard may be down, and there is still time for follow-up questions if it proves an interesting answer.

If an interviewee responds to a question with a question, never answer it. Press for a proper answer if it is needed, but if the question is rhetorical, let the listener answer it while you move on to another area of questioning. Sometimes rhetorical questions can make a good end to an interview.

Use your eyes and facial expression to register understanding, avoiding annoying vocal interjections. Small noises of agreement, unnoticeable in ordinary conversation, can be intensely annoying for the listener.

Be aware of what the interviewee is wearing. Bracelets that jangle or leather jackets that squeak may be very fashionable, but that is not a major consideration on the radio.

If you are doing an interview out in the field, arrange yourself and the interviewee in a sort of 'V' design if you can, because then you can keep both of you on mike without having to move it as much as if you were face to face. Never let an interviewee sit on the other side of a desk. Even if you have arms the length of a gorilla's, the mike lead will suffer from whip-lash.

Always listen to what the interviewee is saying and pick up on it with supplementary questions if necessary. If the interview starts to drift, bring it back on course. Do not allow jargon or technical terms to go unexplained.

When you are getting near the end of the interview, please do not say '... and finally ...'. I have edited tapes that contained as many as three 'and finally's' and have heard presenters do the same on live interviews.

Finish the interview on a high note. People tend to remember what they hear first and last, so make both ends sparkle.

Once you have done the interview, do not let the interviewee listen to it. People tend to want to change something. If *you* are happy with the interview, that is good enough. The only other people who matter at this stage are the editor and the listener.

6

Telling the Story

Story presentation

Your method of presentation may be dictated by the nature of the story or simply by the deadline. Constraints of time may rule out the ideal.

News cuts

The simplest mode of presentation is the news cut, which runs in short news bulletins. That only requires choosing the best short clip of the interview, which could be as short as 10 seconds, or as long as the house style of the station allows, which in IRN's case is 30 seconds. This sounds deceptively simple: remember that the clip must add to the story, be understandable and self-contained, and that the inflections have to be right.

A news cut can also be 'wrapped' (see below, p. 94), with two clips of actuality both introduced and linked by a reporter. Since it still has to be short, the clips will almost certainly be around 10 seconds.

In programme terms, your choice of presentation is broader.

Question and answer (Q & A)

These were traditionally interviews with reporters at the scene of a story, who either hot-foot it into the studio to tell the tale before processing actuality, or explain what is happening from the scene, live on air. The phrase is now often used to describe any interview.

Phone-outs

When a story first breaks, the fastest way to cover it will almost certainly be by telephone. There are other times when phone interviews may be unavoidable, perhaps because the story is happening in a remote area or there is no time to get good quality lines organised. But the simplicity and time-saving qualities of the phone-out may tempt you to use it too often, without considering its disadvantages. The phone line quality makes it that much more difficult for the listener to concentrate on the information. If it is a live phone-out, there is also a danger that the line will deteriorate during the course of the interview. The loss of eye contact can be an added disadvantage, because a person's demeanour can suggest a lot to the interviewer.

If you must cover a story by phone, keep the interview as short as you can while still giving all the essential information. Most producers will only accept a phone quality interview on a local story if it is a major story and there is no other way of covering it. It should be approached as a holding operation that informs the listener quickly. Every effort should be made to get good quality actuality back to base as fast as possible.

Wraps

Most stories have at least two sides to them, and you should present a balanced and comprehensive report. This could be achieved by running a series of Q & As, but that is very time-consuming and probably the least interesting way of presenting a story.

A much better way is to pre-record interviews with all the necessary people and then 'wrap it'. Wraps are the most creative form of presentation, and you can really pack a lot of information into them. While one question and its answer might take a minute of air time, you can get two sides of an issue, plus an explanation of what is going on, into the same amount of time in a wrap.

You can mix sound effects, music and several different participants in your report. Wraps take longer to put together than Q & As, but are a far better listen. You can compress or paraphrase someone's argument, and just use the startling or interesting bit. There may be times when you are unable to get an interview, but the necessary information can be scripted into the wrap so that the report is still fair and balanced.

The interview may happen in a noisy place such as a reception with people talking in the background. Always record at least five minutes' 'wild-tracking', i.e. the sound of the atmospherics at the location of the interview. When you are putting the wrap together in the studio, you can then run the wild-track behind your voice so there is no sudden change of quality. If there does need to be a change in background sounds, let the track run under your voice for a few seconds before fading it out, and then fade in the next track before the next bit of actuality. In that way you can take the listener with you from one location to another.

Put the components of the wrap onto separate carts, so that you can be flexible when deciding the order in which they should appear in the script, and they can be played in without the need to edit gaps when the wrap is being recorded.

An adaptation of the wrap is the 'linked tape' – a short interview with one person as the first band of a tape, and another as the second band, leaving the presenter to link the two live on air.

Vox pops

Vox pops, from the Latin *vox populi* ('voice of the people'), can be lively, interesting little pieces, but you should take care when deciding which issues make good vox pop candidates.

Vox pops are put together by going out on the street to

elicit people's opinions on a subject, then editing them together in sequence so that the question appears only in the cue. They should never be presented as a representative sample. Apart from the obvious fact that you are not presenting a scientifically based report, the whole idea is to pick out the most interesting or lively comments without entirely distorting the general trend of the replies.

The question that elicits the replies must be thought through so that it is easy for people to understand and does not offer them the option of answering with a simple 'yes' or 'no'. If, for example, a report has been published which claims managers are hiring older secretaries who have a wealth of experience rather than attractive young women who can supply cups of tea, a question asking *why* people think this is happening is better than one asking *do* people believe it. Or your question can indicate a more light-hearted approach, such as 'When do you think it appropriate for a manager to make the tea rather than the secretary?'

When the recordings are being made, ask the questions with the recorder on pause and only record people's answers. When the vox is being put together, put the replies you want to use onto carts so that you can start and finish with the best answers. Make those in the middle a good mix of opinions, varying between male and female voices if possible.

Some producers consider that vox pops are a simple and straightforward way to cover a story. They are wrong. Vox pops take up a lot of the reporter's time and are suited to fewer issues than you might imagine.

News presentation

When a story breaks it must be covered. Major stories have a habit of breaking just before bulletins or the start of programmes, forcing you to stretch your resources, skills and intelligence to get them to air fast but accurately.

Remember that 3 words equal 1 second. A 3-minute bulletin equals 540 words – not a lot, which is why IRN has the general rule that cuts have to be a maximum of 30 seconds and wraps no more than 35. Fitting a complex story into 35 seconds will certainly stretch a reporter's writing skills, but spare a thought for the scriptwriter who has to get the story into a two-line headline. Listen to reports on radio and television and analyse the reporters' styles. It will teach you a great deal.

Updating a story is different from 'freshening it up'. Updating involves new material which takes the story further. Freshening is re-writing the same material so it does not sound stale, or presenting an alternative aspect, either in script or in actuality.

Our job is to to convey information clearly and in a way that the listener will understand and want to hear. If we use exactly the same words hour after hour, the listener will become bored and switch off, so freshening up or updating stories is an important part of the job.

News bulletins and news programmes

Journalists who work on the news desk and put together bulletins have the same qualifications as those who work on news programme desks, but they deal with stories differently. For a start, they will have a different idea of who the listener is; in IRN's case, the editors must not think in terms of any particular local audience, even though the bulletin originates from London. It is a national service, so the bulletin has to fit into the programme formats of ILR stations around the country, and the stories must be relevant to everyone.

If a bulletin is a local one, the editor's choice of stories and story order may reflect that to some degree, but the bulletin will still not necessarily sound the same as a news programme. Bulletins are a summary of the news and, in IRN's case, the majority of them must pack the international and national news into 3 minutes. News programmes, on the other hand, can devote more time to explaining the details or background to a story. Even if the format of the programme does not allow tapes to exceed 3½ minutes, that still constitutes more time than the whole of most IRN bulletins.

Partly because of these considerations, there is also a difference in basic news judgments. A bulletin may well lead on events in the Soviet Union on the same day as a news programme leads on the announcement of new rail links for the area. Both stories *may* feature in both bulletins and the programme, but each has different priorities, and the placement of the stories will reflect that. While a bulletin will cover international news, the listener expects a local station to present relevant weather and travel information as well as the local news – indeed, that is one of the strengths of local radio.

There are also differences in style. Even if the same presenter is reading a bulletin and then going on to front a programme, the bulletin will tend to be read straight, without comment or personality. Once the programme gets under way, the presenter's personality and style not only can but must come through.

News judgment

Deciding which items to include in a news bulletin and in what order, or 'news judgment', is largely instinctive and subjective, based on the culture of a newsroom and the perceived audience. While the editors at IRN might each write up a story differently, they would usually agree on the order, or at least the lead story.

The Lockerbie air crash is a good example. Such a major story often completely takes over a bulletin when it first breaks, then dominates bulletins as it moves along, disappearing days later. It will reappear as new angles present themselves, such as when a remembrance service is held for the victims. There will be no disagreement between editors that it is the major story, and little discussion about how long it stays the lead. On days when stories are less obvious, the lead may shift around almost from bulletin to bulletin. Indeed, the various news organisations might each choose a different lead. Those are the days when, in newspaper terms, every paper chooses a different story for its banner headline.

Judgments are made on the basis of an international outlook, but bearing national interests in mind. There is continuing debate about the parochial nature of news, and it is not confined to this country. News – anywhere – must have a parochial element because every story must be relevant to the listener. If three people are killed in a boating accident in Rio de Janeiro, how much does the British listener want to know? It will make a difference if all three are from Manchester.

When deciding how to put together a bulletin, an editor must think about the constraints of time and the mixture of items. There may be a 20-second voice report on a story, but only 12 seconds available for it in the bulletin. The story will have to be rewritten to run as copy, read by the newsreader within the time available. Or there may be four copy stories running one after the other, so a cut is moved from another part of the bulletin in order to break the pattern.

A bulletin editor is to news what a producer is to programmes, only bulletins happen every hour. Every 60 minutes the listener's interest must be re-kindled, so every bulletin must be fresh, carry the information the listener should know, and maintain a good mixture of serious news, off-beat and human interest stories. It is no wonder that editors are voracious beasts, forever on the prowl.

7

Programme Production

The role of the producer

Every aspect of a programme is the final responsibility of the producer. Take other people's opinions and ideas into account as much as you like, but in the end your decision as producer *must* be accepted by everyone else – and if it is wrong, on your head be it. The producer's commitment to the programme differs from that of the other members of the team. Reporters care very much about the items they are responsible for. Presenters care about how the whole programme is put together – after all, they are in the front line when it is on air. But it is the producer who must make all the people and components work well together.

How much planning is long-term and how much short-term is to some extent dictated by the format of a programme. A series or a drama spot can and should be organised well in advance. News and current affairs issues are by definition short-term. How short depends on what it is. If it is a breaking story, be sure it is accurate, but then get it to air fast!

A producer has to have ideas and lots of them. Which ones actually make it must be decided on the basis of the listener finding them interesting or relevant. Even if you are not interested in an item, you decide whether to carry it on the basis of whether people on the top of the bus would be talking about it, or would want to eavesdrop on someone else talking about it. Keep your ears and eyes open – if public transport problems made it difficult for you to get to work, that means the listener also had trouble and will expect you to explain why. Develop at least a curiosity about everything. You may not be interested in sport, or the financial report, or whatever, but the listener is or those spots would not be in the programme.

You must also be well enough informed to be able to decide when an item should stop being run in its specialised spot and start running as general news. Is the winner of the Football League Championship a foregone conclusion, or is it neck and neck, making it worth interviews with the two managers? No subject is boring, but the way it is presented can be.

The producer does not only decide *which* stories to cover, but also *how* to present them and how much weight and time to give to each. When reporters are asked to cover a story, the two questions they ask are 'What angle do you want?' and 'How long should it be?' You can think on your feet to some extent, but you should already have an idea of the story's 'weight' (i.e. is it likely to be a lead or a light tail-ender that will finish the hour) and how much time you think it deserves. Don't be dictatorial. Take the advice of the reporter when the story gets back. It may have turned out to be a cracker, which means you should give the reporter time to dress it up, or it may have ended up dull, in which case drop it and do not waste any more of the reporter's time.

You have a stream of choices as to how to present stories: bring the guest in live during the programme, send a reporter out to do the interview (although even in large stations reporters are a scarce breed), package the item, pre-record a Q & A, etc. If you are producing a phone-in, do you want an expert (e.g. an academic), a pundit (e.g. a journalist who specialises in the subject), or someone with experience of the subject? Which form you opt for depends on the sort of item it is, the programme's format and style, what else is likely to come in, and whether the person you want is free at the necessary or ideal times.

Start out aiming for the ideal, but always stay practical. A great idea may surface, but can your resources stretch far enough to do it justice? Does the idea need to be tailored a bit so it can be done in time? Is it the sort of package you would be better off briefing an outsider to do in order to present you with a finished tape?

Always remember you are a communicator; talk to people about what you're thinking and planning and how you expect them to fit in. Get yourself as familiar with any subject as time will allow and *then* talk to contributors about which areas you are going to cover on air and, sometimes, in what order. A knowledge of at least the basic facts is essential; you cannot speak confidently or authoritatively without it.

You are working with people, so get to know them and their interests. Take in their strengths and weaknesses and use that knowlege in a sensitive but practical way. If, for instance, you know that the guy on the sports desk spends his days off on nature rambles, you could ask his advice about whether an environmental story deserves coverage.

Radio is a *flexible* medium. In the course of every item you put to air, think about ways of brightening it up and making it lively and memorable. As often as possible, think in terms of an outside broadcast (OB). If sound effects bring the item closer, use them. One note of caution, though. Never use any sound effect gratuitously. Use sounds to embellish an item, but do not just throw in a bit of music as a pick-me-up for a programme you think is boring. You have so many choices; never settle for the easy option.

The IBA have become less strict about the separation of editorial material and ads. We do not have to use a sting between an ad sequence and the programme these days, so stings should also be used positively and in a way the listener has come to expect. If your station generally uses stings as an introduction to something, such as news or sports bulletins, do not start throwing them into your programme willy nilly. The presenter should usually be able to separate ads from the programme, but there are occasions when a sting might be appropriate, such as when an ad warning how not to get AIDS is scheduled in a light programme. Even then, think about it in advance, discuss it with your presenter, and try to find a formula that does not prevent the programme being heard as an integrated whole.

Remember that your programme is just part of the station's output: it is not an island, isolated from the rest. So do not end your programme by making it sound as though the station is signing off air (unless it is). Encourage the listener to stay tuned to the programme that follows yours.

Programme preparation

You have decided *what* you are doing and probably *where* most of the items will fit in. Do your final running order in good time, but not until you are pretty sure that things will not change. If you are using a rough running order as a planner coming up to a programme, photocopy the blank *after* you have entered ads and out-times (see below). The location of the ads and the length of the breaks make a big difference to the your timing. The IBA regulations say that there cannot be more than 9 minutes of advertising in each hour, but the ad schedule can vary considerably up to that maximum.

A running order should be detailed enough for any first-timer, whether producer, presenter, or engineer, to be able to walk in and do the programme. On pp. 104-5 there are two running orders: the first is one hour of the *Update* programme that went out on LBC Crown FM, the second is an hour of the *Pete Murray* show on London Talkback Radio.

Update is an afternoon drive-time news magazine programme, while the *Pete Murray* show is a phone-in, so they have very different formats. What each running order has in common, though, is that every sound the listener hears is noted.

Although all the regular items are typed, the daily variations are written in by the producers.

Out-times coming up to the top of the hour are when the presenter must stop speaking so that the newsreader can

UPDATE ... 1600 - 1700   DATE: 22.12.89
NEWS ... Natalie (7.00)
16.07 ... MENU ... Richard and Natalie
          (Richard picks up from news opt)

RUMANIA   IONESCU/PIPER

PARLY   IAN GOW   LIVE
BOX OFFICE ... Natalie   (EX BRIDGE ST)
16.20 ADS:(P10") 30+40
      Travel ... Richard
      ADS:(P10") 30+30
      Update Sting A

WINE   ANDREW JONES
                                        LIVE

OUT TIME: 28'50"
16.28 ADS:(P10") 30+(T)30
      Throw ahead ... Richard
      Station News Sting
16.30 NEWS ... Natalie (4.00)
      Update Sting B

ZOO   SIR ROGER WALTERS
                                        LIVE

16.37 ADS: (P10") 30+30+(T)
      Update Sting A
ARMS/KNGHT   T/C
CRASH/DREERSDEN 1'47"
CRISIS/MULRENNAN   T/C
ALARM/PIPER   1'40"
SANTA/HENLEY   1'15"

16.50 ADS:(P10") 50
      Update Sting B
      Travel ... Richard to introduce Bruce

TV   CHRIS DUNKLEY
                                        LIVE

OUT TIME: 58'40"
16.58 ADS:(P10") 40
59.30 MENU ... Richard
59.50 News Sting
59.55 Pips

0900
IRN + Newslink
SIG BED (Murray v/o menu)
Weather (Murray)
ADS: 30
PROF

GUEST: Jacqui King

ADS: 40 + T

ADS: 30

ADS: 30   OUT TO TRAFFIC 29.20
TRAFFIC STING/BED
AA (40")
ADS: 30

ADS: 60

ADS: 40

TRAFFIC STING/BED   OUT TO TRAFFIC: 57.20
AA (40")
DROP OUT OF PROFANITY (allow 10")
ONE MIN TALK-UP WINDOW
ADS: 40   OUT TO FINAL ADS: 59.10
10" ON HOUR NEWS STING
(fir sting 59'50")

begin exactly on the hour – not a second before or after. There is slightly more flexibility around the out-times for the half-past news summary, but every effort should be made to be as accurate as possible. In either case, the 'hour' is taken for granted, so the times relate to the minutes and seconds.

On *Update*, the running order gives the slug, contributor, and duration of tapes or whether the item is a *live* guest. The cues for each item carry the same information, and each tape is labelled with the date, slug, duration and out-words for that tape. An ROT (Recorded Off Transmission) tape is made of each live guest for possible re-use at a later time, and each ROT is labelled, albeit perhaps with just the name of the contributor, the date, and whether the tape was t/o, or tail-out (most ROTs are, as you do not have time to re-wind the tape once you are in the studio). Cues for live guests are written in advance, and the suggested questions for the presenter cover all the main issues to be discussed.

The information on the *Pete Murray* running order is slightly different. His programme does not usually have taped material, so the producer lists each hour's guest.

It is important that where slugs, durations and out-words appear, they are correct and the same on all related material, i.e. on tape labels, cues and running orders. That is the ideal: there may be circumstances in which it is more important to get the story to air in time than to ensure all that the niceties have been observed. But it is worth making the effort, because consistency in labelling can save mistakes and panics when the programme is going out.

Listen to every tape before it goes to air, not only to check for legals, but also to decide placement. It is dangerous to try to judge from the cue alone, because your final judgment can be swayed by anything from the fact that it is a lively tape to the fact that the quality is just not broadcastable. You also need to listen for pots.

Devise a system of stacking and retrieving tapes that is sensible for your programme, e.g. giving each tape a letter and stacking them in a tray in alphabetical order, or loading items in a tray in the order in which they will run on air. It does not matter how you do it as long as you can lay your hands on a tape quickly if a panic happens in the studio.

Double check out-times *both* before you get into the studio *and* within 20 minutes of getting to them once you are inside. If you are working with an engineer, it is helpful to get a second opinion on your maths.

Finally, be sure that all the principals involved in the programme have a copy of the running order, i.e. presenters, engineers, phone-ops, other producers or anyone else who needs to know what is running in the programme and at what time.

Programme preparation check-list

- All tapes listened through, edited and pot points found.
- Cues checked.
- Running order clearly and fully presented and copied.
- Programme material organised so that it is easy to retrieve.
- Out-times double-checked.
- Be in studio early enough to tidy and equip it, and to test machinery.

Studio production

Being a producer is rather like being a chess player, especially in the studio. You have your pieces (the items for air) and a general game plan (the running order), and you have to think at least three moves ahead.

Ideally you should be in the studio five minutes before the programme starts to check that the microphones are all working, get a voice level from the presenter, make sure talk-back is all right, and generally ensure that all the machinery is working and ready to use. Give yourself ten minutes if the programme is a phone-in because you will need to check that the phone lines are working. The biggest possible panic on a phone-in is a fault on the on-air switchboard. Ensure that you have enough ROT tape and take-up spools, labels and some cue paper.

Be sure your presenter is happy, and has everything he or she needs for the programme. Tidy up the studio if necessary, and check that water is available for the presenter and guests. At this stage, the producer is not just a journalist, but a nurse-maid as well. If the preparation for a programme is thorough and well-organised, and everyone working on it starts out contented and confident, then at least you have a chance of getting through it without panics.

Do not allow lax studio discipline. Any non-essential discussion should take place before or after the programme, not over talk-back during an ad or tape. It is not unknown for a technical fault to send everything said over talk-back to air. This once happened, and was made worse by the nature of the discussion between the presenter and engineer. Everything that is is ever said in front of a mike should be treated as though that mike was 'live' (i.e. switched on).

Before putting any tape to air, listen to the first few words in 'play' mode to ensure:

- it is the right tape
- the cue-in fits
- the technical options are right (tape speed, ½ track, etc).

Before you put a live guest in the studio, run a final check that you have all the details right (name, title, etc) and that your presenter/engineer knows what the stand-by tape is and where it is. You should also have a stand-by ready whenever an item is live. A phone-line or circuit can go down without notice.

Any carts to be used should at least be fast cued to ensure they are properly re-cued. If there is time, play them through at normal speed.

Put each cue in front of you or the engineer as a back-up for when the tape should be fired. Always remember, though, that the end of a scripted cue is only a guide. The tape should be sent to air only when the presenter has given you a visual point cue. Make a note at the top of each cue showing which tape machine that item is on. This should prevent the wrong tape going to air.

Think three moves ahead. For example, the tape on machine 1 is going out, the one on 2 is checked and lined up for air, and now there is time to mosey out to the newsroom and collect the headlines for the half-past summary. Before you leave the control room, be sure both the engineer and the presenter know that the next item is ready. This ensures the smoothest possible gear-change if something goes wrong. If an edit breaks on tape 1, for example, the presenter can apologise and move on without panic to the next item even if the producer is not in the control room to give the instruction. Never leave the presenter abandoned and groping for words because you have not thought far enough ahead.

If there are changes to the running order during the programme (and there often are), tell the presenter on talk-back, then back it up on the VDU screen if you have that facility and *leave it there* until that sequence is finished and you are back to programme as scheduled. If the control room does not have a VDU, confirm what the next item is going to be with the presenter until the programme gets back on course. Change your running order (for the sake of the P as B (see p. 110) as well as keeping it straight) and the engineer's. Remember you are a communicator: tell all the appropriate people what is happening.

If a big story breaks, the newsdesk or reporter should tell the producer, and the producer then tells the presenter and engineer how coverage will be handled. The producer must always be in charge, which means being alert, ahead of the game, informed and confident.

On the cover of *The Hitch-hiker's Guide to the Galaxy* was that 'helpful' instruction, 'DON'T PANIC', which is the producer's golden rule in the studio. If the producer panics, everyone else has no option but to panic as well. Presenters are responsible for making programmes sound smooth and giving the impression that everything is under control. That will not be possible if the production team leaves them in the lurch.

After the programme, tidy up the control room and the studio, check that there are take-up spools on the tape machines and some ROT tape available, and that the studio area is in the state you would like to find it when you arrive.

Finally, sit down and fill out the P as B. This stands for 'Programme as Broadcast' and determines how all the contributors get paid. List everything that went out on the programme, which items need to be paid for, who should be paid and how much. If you used any music in the programme, you must complete a music log so that royalties can be assessed and paid. If you fail to fill out the music log the Performing Right Society will eventually ban the playing of any music on the station as a whole! No producer likes the paper work, but it is a necessary evil.

Programme formats

All programmes must have a format. Because stations break down into departments (programmes, newsroom, sport, etc), we each have a tendency to concentrate on the area we are involved in, but the listener does not. Most of the people who listen to the radio never think about the components involved in what they hear. They hear the station as a whole, and so must you. That includes ads, headlines, fixed spots (which should not be cued as if they were boring time fillers), city and sports reports, etc. All these ingredients are there for positive reasons. You may not be interested, but the listener is.

Time of day is an important consideration in deciding type of programme and format. Early-morning listeners are probably either getting ready for work or travelling to work. Studies indicate that they want, in roughly this order of preference, news, weather, travel information, sport, and time checks. Programmes have to serve up these ingredients regularly, because each listener may tune in for only 30 or 40 minutes, with interruptions for brushing teeth, boiling the kettle, etc. The format of the programme may act as a back-up, or even replacement, for the clock: a commuter may know that by the time a particular sports report begins, he or she should be leaving to catch the train.

By the time 9 or 10 o'clock rolls round, the listener is assumed to be able to give longer spans of attention, so programmes that require more listener involvement can be scheduled. And so on through the day.

In this chapter I will concentrate on magazine programmes and phone-ins because they are the two most common formats used in all-talk broadcasting. But there are other formats which can be programmes in their own right, or be mixed together in some form:

- *Discussion programmes*: a number of participants sit 'round the table' to air different views on an issue, with the presenter as the arbiter or chairman of the discussion.
- *Commentaries*: reporters or presenters describe an event, e.g. a football match, or the ceremony at the Cenotaph on Remembrance Sunday.
- *Drama*: this can be anything from a clever ad to a dramatic reading.
- *Documentaries*: an extended wrap covering different angles of an issue.

Each requires a different approach, but all need a format so that everyone participating in the programme knows where they are at all times – including the listener.

Generally, taking an interview from one programme and dropping it into another does not work, even if the subject matter is similar. For instance, if a news magazine programme did an interview with the Health Minister, what he said in the interview may be relevant to a phone-in programme about health issues, but it might sound odd actually to play it. That is because the presentation styles would be very different, the pace of the two programmes would not be the same, and the formats themselves require different levels of involvement from the listener. These three elements are the basics of any format.

Presentation style

This is the most important feature of any programme because it establishes consistency. The listener gets to know and trust a particular style. Whether a programme maintains and, more important, builds audience figures often depends on whether listeners will accept a specific personality in their homes. They invite you in but can throw you out simply by turning a switch.

It is the job of the programme team to make the presentation style work to its best advantage. That does not mean giving in to a presenter's limitations or allowing the programme to be distorted. It means knowing what material the presenter is naturally comfortable with and when you need to tailor, research or talk through items.

Some people argue that a presenter should write, or re-write, all cues and links so as to maintain an individual style. Whether this is possible depends on the type of programme, the time of day and the presenter. If you end up composing a programme script that someone else is going to read, write it to suit the reader, not to suit you.

Pace

Pace is dictated by both presentation style and the level of listener involvement. A breakfast-time news programme, for example, has a crisp approach and expects the listener to be able to make sharp mental changes of direction, whereas an hour-long phone-in on a single issue expects the listener to concentrate on details. Within a general format pace can be varied for effect, time constraints, or availability of material. Just be aware of what the standard pace is and why you are changing it.

Listener involvement

How much involvement you can demand depends on what the listener is likely to be doing. It would be unreasonable to expect the same level of attention from somone trying to get a family organised and off to school or work as from that same person doing the ironing. The golden rule, however, is one that has been mentioned before: always treat the listener as an *individual*. Do not present your programme to a mass audience, but to one, singular, person.

Magazine programmes

Magazine programmes do not simply consist of a series of individual items, even if the running order makes it look that way. They are integrated programmes made up of linked components. In the same way as you need to 'hear' a cue as you write it, you need to 'hear' a programme as it is set out on a running order. Don't put an item about someone dying of AIDS next to a jokey piece. Stories involving death should be run only among other serious stories, and if a death story is the last in a sequence, pay attention to what sort of ad will follow it. If you are forced to put unsuitable items next to or near each other, the programme team should discuss how to deal with the problem so that the presenter can cope once the programme is on air.

The presenter of a magazine programme needs to integrate the components to keep the programme flowing as a whole. Tapes should not be treated as though they had dropped in from another planet, but reacted to in the same way as a live interview. If, for instance, there is a light-hearted tape going out on air, and the presenter back-announces it in a dry, straightforward manner, that will have a jarring effect on the listener.

A bit of thought as to placement and perhaps the addition of a phrase to the top of a cue can work wonders in terms of integrating items in a programme. Say you are kicking off a programme hour with a report from Washington on

President Bush's difficulties in getting Congress to approve his candidate for appointment as Defense Secretary, followed by a tape about the latest problems President Gorbachev is having with his Glasnost policies. On paper, you might start out without any scripted back-anno for the Washington piece, and the start of the Moscow cue might be: 'In Moscow, Mikhail Gorbachev is being confronted with another challenge to his plans for a more open structure for Soviet society – or Glasnost.'

If you now insert at the top of the Moscow cue: 'Nick Peters reporting from Washington. And while President Bush is wrestling with his Congress, the leader of the other superpower is having to deal with problems of his own,' you will have achieved two ends. The Washington tape has been back-announced, and a bridge has been formed to the next item.

Be careful not to misuse or overdo these sorts of links. If a story is completely unrelated to the previous item, tell the listener so by using the right words and voice inflection.

You need to take the listener with you from item to item. Signpost changes of direction, and try to keep the sequence as logical as possible.

When you are cueing up live interviews, you must have some idea of what each answer will be in order to keep it logical. Sometimes the only way to achieve this is by having a 'pre-interview interview' on the phone. Contributors tend to appreciate such chats because it gives them some idea of the areas you want to cover.

The programme should be organised flexibly so that the format works for you rather than you slaving away to it. Do not let the format force you to run certain tapes at certain times. To return to the example of the two tapes from Moscow and Washington, you might have decided to run Washington as your lead at the top of the hour, and then use the Moscow tape as the lead after the headlines at half past the hour. Many news magazines use the second lead at the half hour in order to spread the interest and weight through the hour.

Each programme should, in a sense, emulate something

like a spinach and bacon salad. The spinach is tasty but soft, and every now and then you come across a bit of crisp, salty bacon. Every item in the programme should be able to stand on its own in terms of relevance and interest, but the listener should not be bombarded with a sequence of tapes that are all too similar in subject or style of presentation. Try to achieve an interesting mix of Q & As, wraps, live interviews, etc, that still allow the programme to flow.

You should have time in the planning stage of the programme to make a cool calculation of what sort of news day it is going to be. If it is a bad one, you will end up going for stories that you would normally never consider. If a big story is breaking, it will dominate the programme and other news will need to be edited down to fit into whatever crevices are left. Make life easier for yourself by doing as much as possible as early as possible. That way, if a story breaks just before the programme goes to air you will be able to concentrate on it rather than on the material you could have processed an hour before.

Initiate more stories than you have space for. There are two reasons for doing this. First, there will always be some stories that do not materialise for one reason or another. Secondly, as a former editor of ITN put it, any programme is only as good as what has been left out. So if your programme usually requires a dozen items to fill it, initiate at least fifteen.

Magazine programmes tend to present a slice of life. Each programme should reflect a healthy personality, with a good general mix of serious and light items, art, sport, money interests, etc. The listener may not be an expert in every field, but will probably be an armchair *aficionado* in at least one, and interested in them all.

Phone-ins

Phone-ins may seem easier to put together than magazines. Only one item has to be set up, and the callers do a lot of the hard work by deciding what questions to put. Unfortunately, however, phone-ins can be much more stressful.

For a start, you do not have the cushion of setting up more items than you need. Finding the right person, who is free to discuss the subject at the right time, can be a nightmare. You are also dependent on the callers' active involvement. It is difficult to have a good phone-in when no one rings up.

As to the subjects, which ones spark interest is always a wonder. How the police carry out their duty, for example, is an important issue which affects people's lives, but the subject seldom provokes a lively response. But ask Harry Feigen of the Licensed Taxi Drivers Association to come in, for no particular reason, and the board lights up (see the warning on consumer issues, p. 120). Everyone, it seems, has an opinion on the taxi service and how good it is, but people are happy to let police officers police themselves.

Phone-ins are a little slice of democracy, letting the listener finally have a say on the issues of the day, or even complain about an aspect of the station's output. That's fine, but the listener's contribution must come from an acceptable source.

Calls from phone boxes should not be allowed on air because call boxes are largely for people to use in an emergency. A contributor to a phone-in could tie up a call box for ten minutes or more. There is no way of checking whether a call box is in someone's house, so it is a blanket ban. Phonecards and the new-style phones make it more difficult to recognise instantly whether a call emanates from a phone box, but use your ears and try to establish that the call is from a personal phone.

It is against the law to drive and speak into a hand-held mobile phone. You must be sure that the caller has pulled over and stopped before taking the call. And that means they have to stop legally. A caller's contribution was once halted prematurely because he had stopped on the hard shoulder of a motorway: he had to stop speaking to the programme and start speaking to the policeman.

There are also technical reasons for being tough on callers from both phone boxes and car phones. Calls from phone boxes inevitably go to air just as the pips sound and the money runs out. Car phones offer what can only be called 'variable' line quality so even if the caller is a passenger, do not take the call until they have pulled over. The sound of the programme comes first, and keeping a phone-in on course and interesting is hard enough without inviting problems.

Five questions must be answered positively before taking any call:

- Is the line broadcastable? No matter how good a point is, if it is inaudible it is a non-point. Ask the caller to ring back, or take the number and ring back. If it is an interesting point, keep trying until you get a decent line.
- Is the caller coherent? If the person is inarticulate to the point of being unable to make a clear point, the pace of the programme will be destroyed while the presenter tries to hack through the morass. People who are a bit tipsy are dangerous, so keep the contribution short and your finger over the prof button. Those who have had so much to drink as to put them into the inarticulate category should not be inflicted on the sober listener.
- Is the point relevant? People's ideas of what areas are associated with any subject never cease to amaze me. Someone must keep them to the point, and it is better if that person is the producer rather than the presenter. If the programme is taking general callers, specialised questions should not get through: a presenter is not a specialist.
- Is there sufficient time to deal with the point? It is frustrating if there is less than a minute left before the programme ends and an interesting point needing two minutes has to be cut short. Better to take details of the call and start a subsequent programme with it.
- Is the caller able to hang on until the presenter is ready? Unlike the BBC, we do not call back every contributor, and it can cause bedlam in the control room and possible confusion on air if a caller hangs up just as the presenter gets to that line. But if you know that a caller is likely to have to wait for ten minutes or more before actually

getting to air, it is only fair to ring him or her back. You don't want to put people off ringing in because their phone bills are rocketing.

Life is made much easier if your station has VDU screens that link the control room with the presenter. Details of who has called, what about and in what order calls should be taken can be 'stacked' on the screen. Regardless of how the control room communicates with the studio, however, before any details go up on the screen or its equivalent you must ensure the following:

- There is a clear understanding of what the caller wants to say.
- All the details have been entered on the phone log, i.e. the caller's name, the area he or she is calling from (if relevant), the topic to be discussed, and the caller's telephone number. Without the first and last of those, you are in breach of IBA guidance.
- The caller's radio is either off or far enough away not to be heard. Callers get desperately confused if they can hear the radio. The programme is going out in delay, so they hear themselves up to ten seconds after they have actually spoken, and callers inevitably listen to the radio rather than the phone.
- The caller agrees to hold on unless you agree that you will phone back.
- The caller is properly switched through to air and standing by.

These steps are usually short-circuited when there is a shortage of calls, although that is exactly when they ought to be strictly adhered to. If the presenter has been filling air time, waiting longer than usual for someone to call, it is understandable that the caller may get on air before all the details are in front of the presenter.

Telephone log sheets should at least contain the caller's name, telephone number, and which line they have phoned in on. The IBA says the logs should be kept 'for a time' in case there is a need to get back to someone, whether for legal or other reasons. Phone logs are always confidential unless the programme format makes it obvious to callers that their number will be made available to other callers.

Phone-ops should be briefed carefully. They are your first line of defence, so be sure they know what sort of calls you are willing to take on any programme or subject. Phone-ops have arguably the worst job in a radio station. It is hard enough for them to deal with the punters; don't make the job worse by being vague.

General open line

You need to give the listeners some idea of the range of subjects you would like to cover at the start of the programme, and also indicate whether they will be allowed to introduce subjects. Consider the parameters you would apply in ideal circumstances, but if the calls are slow, shelve the ideal world and broaden your horizons. There are times when a caller will introduce a subject out of the blue that will virtually take over the programme. Just hope that the subject is interesting and fun, and not yet another discussion on an issue that has already been talked to death. My heart still sinks if anyone wants to talk about the pros and cons of the Wapping dispute, and it has to be a particularly dull day for either dog licences or pensions to be inspiring subjects.

The producer and presenter should have discussed enough possible ideas and angles for callers to consider so that the presenter is not left floundering. Organising the format so there is a break between the introductory remarks and taking the first call creates a bit more time for the listener to get through.

As in all other types of programme, but especially phone-ins because they are continuously live, producers should never leave presenters in the dark. Let the presenter know if the phone panel is busy but full of cranks, or if calls are slow, or they are all labouring a point that has already been made. The presenter is in a position to do something positive about the problem: 'I think we've pretty much dealt with the Wapping dispute for the time being, but I'd be interested in what you think about this morning's assassination of the American President.'

Develop an antenna that is always up. Non-broadcasters are going to air and there is just no telling what they might come out with. You need to have a sixth sense that warns you when someone is straying into a dangerous area.

Specific subject with guest

Remember the listener: does anybody care about the issue? If so, is it a topic people will have something to say about?

Any 'expert' you have not heard on air before should be taken through a thorough pre-booking chat about the area you want to cover. Be sure you have the right person who can talk well. Be sure that person is capable of fielding a wide range of questions.

Don't commit yourself when you first contact a possible guest. Say something along these lines: 'We're thinking about doing a programme on ——, and I wondered if I could ask you a few questions about it.' You can then have a conversation about the subject, and if your expert turns out to have a stammer or a thick Yugoslavian accent, you can gracefully exit.

Explain to every guest that it is a phone-in and how callers get to air (i.e. what sort of screening process takes place). If the subject you want to discuss has two sides to it (and most do), decide whether to have both sides represented or do a follow-up programme later. Set up both sides before airing one, and tell both guests what you are doing.

Be careful about setting up consumer specialities. Such programmes often create a lot of listener interest, which is the point of the exercise, but can lead to a string of complaints too specific for any other listener to relate to. Besides, the advice tends to be much the same for everybody.

Profanity

The red button is used more for libel and contempt than for four-letter words. It is fair enough for someone to complain about the standards of consumer items, say, but not specifically a particular pen company being in cahoots with a clothing-maker because their pens inevitably leak in your inside pocket (which Spike Milligan once did during a live interview when we were not in prof). If a dodgy comment slips through the net, get rid of the offending call and distance the station from the statement ('Come on, millions have chosen that product. I'm sure if you have a particular complaint, you'll write to the company. We'll leave you to get on with your letter while we talk to …')

Biro, Kleenex and Hoover have become generic terms for ball-point pens, paper tissues and vacuum cleaners, but that does not save you from libel. If a company or brand name is used you are on dangerous ground.

8

The Law and the Courts

Introduction

Most of us never get involved with the law and therefore
know little about it. There is a sort of received wisdom that
everything to do with the law is complicated and difficult to
understand. While this may be so in some areas, generally
the law and the way the administration of justice functions
are logical and have more to do with common sense than
you might expect.

In this book I deal with the law of England and Wales.
Scottish law and its administration differ in many ways
from the rest of the UK, and if you are working in Scotland
you will need to familiarise yourself with those differences.
The Law Society of Scotland (Rutland Exchange Box EDI,
26 Drumsheugh Gardens, Edinburgh EH3 7YR) has a
helpful typewritten summary, and HMSO publish a good
basic guide, *The Legal System of Scotland* (but be aware of
the fact that some details are now out-of-date).

Lawyers often use very precise language which is either
not English or old-fashioned English. I have tried to
translate legal terminology into 'ordinary' English when it
occurs. If I have failed to define any legal term, a good
dictionary will explain it. The precision of legal language
extends to the particular wording of a law, so it is
important to read each word carefully.

Be sure that you understand these chapters on the law. As
a journalist you have no special rights or privileges, so it is
important to keep within the law and have it on your side.

Divisions of the law

The criminal law deals with *offences*. When you see a case referred to as *R* v *Smith* it means that the state is prosecuting the case, the *R* standing for *Rex* or *Regina* (depending on whether it is in the reign of a king or queen) who is versus (against) Smith. Criminal cases must be proved 'beyond reasonable doubt'. They are *prosecuted* and the guilty *punished*, e.g. by a fine, imprisonment or probation.

There are two elements in most crimes: a criminal act and a guilty intent. Without intent, no crime is committed, unless the crime is 'absolute' (i.e. no intent is required, as in jumping a red light) or intent is presumed because it occurred through recklessness (as when an accident is caused by a speeding driver).

The civil law deals with claims of either a private or a public nature to remedy *wrongs*. Cases are referred to as, for example, *Brown* and *Smith*. The *plaintiff* (Brown) *sues* the *defendant* (Smith) who may be *found liable*. If you find it difficult to remember what each side is called, you may find it helpful to remember that it is the *plaint*iff who is making the com*plaint*. Civil cases must be proved 'on a balance of probability', which is less onerous than in criminal courts.

Types of courts

All cases must follow a prescribed route through the courts. A case starts in the lower courts, and may then progress through to successively higher courts as shown below.

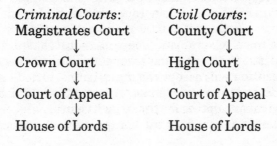

Criminal Courts:	*Civil Courts*:
Magistrates Court	County Court
↓	↓
Crown Court	High Court
↓	↓
Court of Appeal	Court of Appeal
↓	↓
House of Lords	House of Lords

Criminal courts

Magistrates Courts

All criminal cases start in the Magistrates Courts, which always make the initial decisions about whether bail and/or legal aid will be granted, although lawyers sometimes challenge those decisions in a higher court. Most relatively minor cases do not proceed to a higher court.

Magistrates are usually lay men and women who rely on the clerk of the court to advise them on the law, but there are also legally qualified stipendiary magistrates who sit in some courts in larger cities. While lay magistrates usually sit in twos or threes, stipendiaries sit on their own. All magistrates are Justices of the Peace (JPs).

Cases in the Magistrates Courts fall into one of three categories:

- *Summary trials.* 'Summary' means that the case must be heard in the Magistrates Court and cannot proceed to the Crown Court. These cases are relatively minor, e.g. disorderly conduct or obstructing the highway. Magistrates can impose a maximum of 6 months imprisonment and/or a £2000 fine, but they can refer a case up to the Crown Court for sentencing if the defendant is found guilty and they feel a tougher sentence is in order. Unless the magistrate is a stipendiary (i.e. legally qualified), at least two magistrates must sit in summary trials.
- *Triable either way*, e.g. most offences of theft, damaging property, arson, bigamy, etc. The prosecution will first say where they think a case should be heard. If it is serious (e.g. theft of £10,000), the prosecution will opt for the Crown Court, and the magistrates will 'decline jurisdiction'. If the theft is of a can of beans, the prosecution will accept the magistrates' jurisdiction, but the defendant can exercise the right to trial by jury, which means opting for the Crown Court.
- *Indictable only*, e.g. murder, rape. Serious charges must

be tried by a jury, but these cases still pass through the Magistrates Court.

Committal proceedings

Any case that is progressing beyond the Magistrates Court must go through committal proceedings. In these cases, the role of the magistrates is to decide whether there is a case to answer, i.e. whether the prosecution's evidence is strong enough.

A *paper committal* means that the prosecution and the defence agree that there is a case to answer based on papers served by the prosecution on the defence. This procedure was brought in to reduce the number of lengthy committal proceedings.

In an *old style committal* the defence insists that the prosecution present all or part of their evidence in open court in order to determine whether there is a case to answer. If the magistrates decide that there is, the case is sent to the Crown Court. If not, the defendant is discharged. In the latter case it is wrong to say that the defendant was 'found innocent'; you can say that the person was 'released' or 'discharged'.

If someone is accused of serious fraud the case can be given a 'certificate' by the prosecution which will transfer it directly to the Crown Court without a lengthy committal.

The Magistrates Courts Act 1980 lays down strict reporting restrictions on all cases in the Magistrates Courts (see p. 156) unless it is the actual hearing of a summary case.

Crown Courts

Crown Court judges are always legally qualified with at least ten years' experience and, unless they are hearing submissions or dealing with matters from the Magistrates Courts (e.g. sentencing), they sit with a jury. So long as reports are within the bounds of contempt of court (see p. 156), restrictions do not generally apply unless a judge specifically orders them.

There are eleven Crown Courts in London, including the Old Bailey, or Central Criminal Court. Cases can be transferred to the Old Bailey for security reasons, or because a defendant is thought to be unable to get a fair trial at a local Crown Court because of the strength of local opinion.

Circuit judges sit in criminal cases, while High Court judges can hear either criminal or civil cases. If it is a serious case, whether in the Old Bailey or any other crown court, a High Court judge may hear the case.

Court of Appeal

This court hears appeals from the Crown Courts only on points of law against conviction, or against sentence. Once a jury has heard and decided on a particular case, the Court of Appeal will be reluctant to overturn the jury's decision, as in the cases of the Guildford Four or the Birmingham Six. But if the trial judge misdirected the jury on a point of law, or if the Court decides that fresh evidence might have brought a jury to a different conclusion, the Appeal Court can overturn a conviction, or more rarely order a re-trial.

It is not so unusual for the Court to hear appeals against sentence. If the defence thinks the sentence was too severe, an application can be made to the Court of Appeal to have it reduced, but the Court does have the option of increasing the sentence if it is so minded.

Only the defence can appeal against conviction, but either side can appeal against sentence. The Attorney General used his powers under the Criminal Justice Act 1988 for the first time in August 1989 when he appealed against a three-year sentence given to a man found guilty of indecent assault on his daughters. The Court of Appeal doubled the sentence and laid down guidelines for future sentencing in similar cases.

The prosecution can appeal against an acquittal, but the appeal must come from the Attorney General and the Court of Appeal's decision will not alter the trial court's outcome.

Thus the Court can deliberate on the general issues of a case, but cannot fine or jail the particular defendant.

Three appeal judges hear each case, and the majority decision is binding.

The Court of Appeal is usually the last opportunity to challenge a decision, because very few cases are accepted by the Lords.

House of Lords

Appeals only get to the Lords if they involve points of law that are of general public importance. The Lords will not hear a case unless both of those requirements have been met.

Cases are not heard by the whole House of Lords. There are nine Lords of Appeal who are paid, professional judges, holding life peerages. Five Lords hear each case, and a majority decision is binding.

Both the Court of Appeal and the House of Lords are said to 'grant leave to appeal', which means they have decided to hear the case. Otherwise 'leave is refused'.

Civil courts

County Courts

County Court judges sit on their own. They are legally qualified, and full judges must have at least 10 years' experience. County Courts deal with cases concerning less than £5000 claimed, or property valued at less than £30,000. Day-to-day cases are dealt with here, and County Courts deal with about 90 per cent of civil cases. The range of cases they hear is very broad, but a large part of their work involves landlord-and-tenant disputes and debt.

High Court

The High Court usually sits in the Royal Courts of Justice in the Strand, London. The judge sits alone, except for certain appeals, and his decision is not generally given directly the case finishes, but 'handed down' at some later date when he has considered the arguments. The decision is handed down in writing to the interested parties rather than spoken in court.

The High Court deals with cases involving sums higher than the County Courts can hear, and some sorts of cases, e.g. libel, start in the High Court.

While most cases are heard in London, High Court judges also 'go on circuit' and hear cases in other major cities.

Court of Appeal

This court also sits in the Royal Courts of Justice in the Strand. Appeals are generally heard by three judges, and the majority ruling is binding. They hear appeals from the County and High Courts, and from employment tribunals.

House of Lords

As in criminal cases, the Lords grant leave only on points of law that are of general public importance.

Judges' titles

Depending on seniority, different judges are referred to in particular ways.

- Magistrates are referred to as Mr, Mrs or Miss Smith.
- County Court judges are referred to as Judge Smith.
- Crown Court circuit judges are initially referred to as Judge John Smith, then subsequently as Judge Smith. High Court judges are Mr, Mrs or Miss Justice Smith.
- In the Court of Appeal, whether it is a civil or criminal case, judges are referred to as Lord Justice Smith. The title of Lord Justice applies to women as well as men.
- Regardless of whether it is a civil or criminal case, judges in the House of Lords are referred to as Lord Smith.

Solicitors and barristers

Lawyers are either solicitors or barristers. Both are legally trained, but they perform different functions.

Solicitors see clients first and assess their cases. They can take advice from barristers at any stage, but it is the job of the solicitor to deal generally with the case and prepare it for court. They negotiate with 'the other side' when appropriate, decide which laws and precedents are pertinent, arrange witnesses and plan the trial strategy.

There are rules about which courts solicitors are allowed 'a right of audience' in, i.e. which courts allow them to speak. They are confined to speaking in the lower courts, such as Magistrates Courts, County Courts and tribunals. There are circumstances in which they are allowed to speak to a Crown Court, but generally they have to 'brief' a barrister for that stage.

In criminal cases, solicitors for the defence are usually in private practice, while those for the prosecution are usually part of the state Crown Prosecution Service or CPS.

Solicitors can practise alone or in partnerships. Barristers, on the other hand, are always self-employed and organise themselves to share 'chambers' (their office) and 'clerks' (who run their office).

Barristers (also called 'counsel') cannot solicit work directly from members of the public, and can only get their briefs from solicitors. They have a right of audience in all courts, although when they appear in Magistrates Courts, they do not wear black gowns and white wigs. Those come into play once a case gets to the Crown Court. Judges also wear gowns and wigs, although more senior judges' robes are red. When barristers have distinguished themselves in practice for a number of years, they may be appointed as a 'Queen's Counsel', or QC. QCs are always barristers.

A barrister may work closely with a solicitor in the planning of a case, or, if it is a straightforward hearing, may present the case simply on the basis of having read the documents.

Once a case gets to the Crown Court, the solicitor, or a

representative of the solicitor, must always 'sit behind' counsel – a literal description of their respective positions.

Solicitors are answerable to the Law Society, while the equivalent for barristers is the Bar Council (when barristers qualify, they are 'called to the Bar').

During the course of a case, or at the end of it, the solicitor can make statements or be interviewed. Most barristers, however, refuse to talk about a case in which they are involved, and confine themselves to speaking about general issues of law.

That is how the system works at the moment, but as this book went to press the Lord Chancellor was seeing a new law through Parliament that will substantially alter the legal profession. The Courts and Legal Services Bill will bring in new rules governing the rights of audience so that some solicitors can conduct cases in the higher courts. Solicitors who have acquired full rights of audience for the requisite number of years would be eligible to become judges.

Multi-Disciplinary Practices (MDPs) are also under consideration. If they are accepted, a combination of solicitors and barristers will be allowed to set up in business together. This proposal has been criticised by all sectors of the legal profession.

The proposals also call for two new bodies to be convened. The Lord Chancellor's advisory committee will advise him on maintaining standards of conduct and competence in the profession, and there will be a new joint disciplinary body (comprised of members of the Bar, the Law Society and possibly the judiciary) to deal with complaints about court work.

Court procedure

Criminal courts

The basic procedure in criminal courts is as follows:

1. The accused is read the charges ('charged' in Magistrates Courts; 'arraigned' in Crown Courts, which

means it is an 'indictable' case) and asked to plead guilty or not guilty. If the plea is guilty points 2-7 are omitted. If not guilty:

2. The prosecution opens the case with a speech, then calls witnesses (who can be cross-examined by the defence) to prove the case.

3. The defence makes an opening statement, then calls witnesses (who can be cross-examined by the prosecution).

4. The prosecution makes a closing speech (except in the Magistrates Courts where the prosecution only replies to points of law).

5. The defence makes a closing speech.

6. (In jury trials only) the judge sums up the evidence and instructs the jury on points of law before the jury retire to consider their verdict.

7. If the defendant is found innocent he is aquitted. If he is found guilty or pleaded guilty in the first place (see 1 above):

8. The prosecution outlines relevant criminal records, reports, etc.

9. The defence sets out pleas in mitigation (reasons why the defendant should not get the harshest penalty).

10. Sentence is passed.

At the end of the prosecution's case (point 4 above), the defence may claim there is 'no case to answer'. If the court accepts this application, the case is *discharged*.

A jury is made up of 12 people, but if for some reason one, or even two, need to drop out during the course of a trial, the case will probably carry on so as not to cause the defendant the added stress of having to start all over again. The jury may agree a unanimous verdict, but if they are unable to agree, a majority verdict of 11-1 or 10-2 can be accepted by the judge. If the jury has been reduced, the judge can accept a 10-1 or 9-1 decision.

If a defendant is convicted by a majority jury decision, you can say so; but it is regarded as bad form to say that an acquittal was by majority (it suggests that some jurors thought the defendant was guilty).

Civil courts

The order in civil cases is similar:

1. The plaintiff's lawyer may make an opening speech (but this is not mandatory).
2. The plaintiff's lawyer calls witnesses (who can be cross-examined by the defence).
3. The defence lawyer makes an opening speech.
4. The defence calls witnesses (who can be cross-examined by the plaintiff's lawyer).
5. The defence lawyer makes a closing speech.
6. The plaintiff's lawyer makes a closing speech.
7. (In jury trials only) the judge sums up the evidence and directs the jury on points of law.
8. The judgment is given.

Types of crime

Never ascribe the wrong charge to a defendant. If, for example, you say someone is accused of robbery when in fact it is theft, expect a call from the defending lawyer, because you have just accused the defendant of a more serious crime than the prosecution has. These are some of the more newsworthy charges you may come across:

Crimes against the person

- Murder: killing with malice aforethought. Carries a mandatory life sentence.
- Manslaughter: killing without malice aforethought.
- Suicide: ceased to be a crime in 1961, but it is still a crime to assist suicide, unless it is a suicide pact.
- Infanticide: killing of a baby by its mother, whose responsibility may be reduced because her mind is disturbed by the stress of the birth.
- Assault: an act which puts someone in fear of an attack.
- GBH (grievous bodily harm): an attack with intent to cause serious bodily harm (maximum sentence life imprisonment).

- Malicious wounding: carries a sentence of up to 5 years imprisonment.
- ABH (actual bodily harm): not as serious as GBH.
- Rape: sexual intercourse with penetration with a woman without her consent.
- Unlawful sexual intercourse: intercourse with a girl under 16.
- Indecent assault: an assault involving indecency (but not rape) which can be committed by a male or female against either sex, but if the person is under 16, consent is no defence.

Crimes against property

- Theft: stealing something with the intent of permanently depriving the owner.
- Robbery: theft by force or threat of force.
- Burglary: trespassing into a building and stealing or committing GBH, or intending to steal, or commit GBH, or rape.
- Aggravated burglary: armed burglary.
- Obtaining property by deception: can be called fraud.
- Obtaining a pecuniary advantage by deception: can also be called fraud (an example is someone obtaining an overdraft by deception).
- Blackmail: an 'unwarranted' demand with menaces.
- Handling: receiving, keeping or disposing of goods knowing or suspecting them to be stolen, or assisting another to do so.
- TCA: taking a car without authority (used to be known as taking and driving away, or TDA): not to be confused with theft. You can say the car was taken for a joy ride, but *not* stolen.

Motoring offences

- Causing death by reckless driving (maximum sentence 5 years)
- Reckless driving: driving without regard for other road users.

- Careless driving: driving without due care and attention. Less serious than reckless driving.
- Driving while unfit through drugs or drink.
- Driving over the limit: driving with excess alcohol in the blood.

New motoring laws are being discussed in Parliament which will change some offences and maximum sentences.

Tribunals and inquiries

The workings and decisions of tribunals and inquiries are often newsworthy. They tend to operate in a less formal way than the courts, which can make reporting them easier. There are hundreds of different sorts of tribunals, each with its own working practices and powers, ranging from Mental Health Review Tribunals, which decide whether a person should be compulsorily detained under the Mental Health Act, to professional bodies, which can fine or suspend their members, to public inquiries held to investigate and report on the causes of major accidents. There is even a Wireless Telegraphy Tribunal, though it has never been convened since its inception in 1949.

Most tribunals and inquiries operate under quasi-legal procedures and your coverage of them will fall within privilege, although it will be qualified privilege in most cases (see p. 148). They tend to be open to the public and press, except for hearings into the misconduct of members of some professions (including the medical and legal professions), Mental Health Review Tribunals and Supplementary Benefit Tribunals. It is not clear whether tribunals and inquiries are legally courts and therefore covered by the rules of contempt, but practice and rulings to date suggest that contempt does not apply in most instances.

The only tribunals for which legal aid is available are the Mental Health Review Tribunal and the Lands Tribunal. For all the others, clients can get legal advice on legal aid, but the state will not pay for a lawyer to present the case itself. Given the complexity of the law covered by many tribunals, this has been heavily criticised. The body that keeps tribunals under review, the Council on Tribunals, has pressed governments for many years to extend legal aid, but so far without success.

The most likely sources of interesting stories are industrial tribunals, planning inquiries and public inquiries.

Industrial tribunals

Industrial tribunals decide on a wide range of employment matters, including claims of unfair dismissal, redundancy pay, sexual or racial discrimination, and issues relating to trade union representation. Three people hear cases: a chairperson (who is legally trained), a representative of a trade union and a representative of industry, although their affiliations are not made public.

Appeals go to the Employment Appeal Tribunal where a High Court judge sits with at least two lay people.

Planning inquiries

If for any reason a local authority refuses permission for land development or a change of its use, the applicant is entitled to a planning inquiry. Objectors are entitled to an inquiry only if the Secretary of State agrees to allow one, or if the objectors can show that a national issue is involved.

Strictly speaking, it is the Secretary of State for the Environment who takes the final decision on disputed planning appeals, but an inspector is usually appointed to head the inquiry, and the inspector will hear arguments from the applicant and objectors and then present recommendations to the Secretary of State, or, in some cases, decide the issue. The only appeal is by submission to the Secretary of State.

Public inquiries

A major disaster or crisis will often provoke a public

inquiry. These may be set up by a government department (as with the Zeebrugge ferry disaster), or by a private organisation (e.g. the National Council for Civil Liberties' inquiry into the death of Blair Peach). Public inquiries tend to be quasi-judicial in nature, but the legal powers available to them depend upon how they were constituted in the first place. Royal Commissions and departmental inquiries command far more powers than private inquiries, which depend on the good will of participants.

Public inquiries produce reports from which the government decides whether to take any further action.

Coroner's Courts

If a death is unnatural, violent or sudden, a coroner's inquest must be held. If the autopsy subsequently shows that the person died of natural causes, the coroner can dispense with the inquest.

A coroner can be a barrister, solicitor or doctor of at least five years' standing. If the coroner is not legally qualified, the inquest will be assisted by a policeman who acts as the 'coroner's officer'.

The coroner can decide whether to have a jury unless the death was in prison, by poison or in circumstances prejudicial to public safety, in which case a jury must sit. Juries consist of between 7 and 11 members, and they *return* a verdict. If the coroner is sitting without a jury, a verdict is *recorded*.

If a crime is associated with the death, the coroner will formally open an inquest and then adjourn it until after any proceedings involved in the crime have finished.

Inquests are always open to reporters and the general public, unless considerations of national security make it necessary to hold the inquest *in camera* (in secret).

Coroner's Courts are inquisitorial rather than accusatorial. The coroner does not act as an impartial judge. He or she decides which witnesses should be called and leads the parties through their testimony. Lawyers for interested parties can be present and can be allowed to ask questions, but they do not make opening or closing statements.

The purpose of the inquest is to establish the identity of the person who has died, and how, when and where the death occurred. If a jury is hearing the case, they can only return a verdict on how the death occurred. They are not allowed to name anyone in connection with murder or manslaughter. Until 1980 they were allowed to add a rider to their verdict in order to suggest ways of preventing further such deaths, but that right has now been taken away.

Reports of coroner's inquests carry the protection of absolute privilege (see p. 147).

Treasure trove

If gold or silver is found and the rightful owners or their descendants cannot be established, a coroner's inquest will be opened to decide whether the person who found it can keep it, or whether it is *treasure trove*. Treasure trove is the property of the Crown.

The definition of treasure trove is property which the last owner intended to recover. If it was deliberately abandoned or accidentally lost, it is not treasure trove. So, for instance, if coins are found at the site of an ancient religious site or burial ground, and the prevailing view is that those coins were sacrifices or offerings, it is unlikely that they would be deemed treasure trove.

Since the advent of metal detectors, there has been a spate of treasure trove cases, and they are almost always good human interest stories. The reason these cases are heard in the Coroner's Court reflects the original purpose of the coroner: to protect the Crown's financial interests.

European courts

European courts can influence British courts, but courts in this country must always follow British law. There are two European courts which influence our laws. Their proceedings are *not* covered by privilege (see p. 145).

- *The European Court of Justice* is part of the EEC, and it will hear only cases that have been referred to it by a member state. Its decisions are binding on British courts, but only cases which involve questions of European law are heard here.
- Newsworthy cases often find their way to the *European Court of Human Rights*, which is part of the Council of Europe. The decisions of this court are not strictly speaking binding on British courts, but since this country is a signatory to the Convention on Human Rights, the government has a responsibility to amend the law in accordance with its findings.

If a defendant claims that any section of the Convention has been contravened, the European Commission of Human Rights will consider the case only when all domestic remedies have been exhausted (i.e. the case has failed in all possible appeals, right up to the House of Lords). If the Commission agrees that the defendant has a possible case, it will invite both sides to try to find a mutually agreed conclusion. Failing an agreement, the Commission may pass on the case to be heard in full in the European Court of Human Rights.

Alternatively, if there is no domestic remedy available, a case can be started by the defendant making a complaint (or submission) in writing directly to the Commission. If the Commission accepts that the complaint is worth consideration, it will first invite the two sides to try to work out a solution. If no solution is forthcoming, the issue will go to the Court of Human Rights to be heard in full. This is the process that has been instigated by Times Newspapers in their petition regarding libel damages (see p. 154), because there is no legal process available in this country to hear or decide the issue.

9

Libel

Libel is dealt with by two main statutes, the Law of Libel Amendment Act 1888 and the Defamation Act 1952. In 1975 the Faulks Committee on Defamation published its report, making recommendations for changes in the law, most of which have not been taken up. The courts mainly rely on previous cases (precedents) for guidance, while looking at each case on its own merits. Juries decide on the outcome of each case and the amount of damages that should be awarded, and they sometimes come to unexpected decisions.

The courts themselves recognise the complexities of the laws of libel. In a judgment handed down in May 1989, Lord Justice May said that Appeal Court judges 'had with increasing frequency complained of the unnecessary complication and obscurity of rules of pleading in defamation cases', and called for the law to receive 'swift and firm consideration by the Law Commission and the Supreme Court Rules Committee'. However, the only aspect of libel that has evoked any firm reaction is that of the awarding of damages (see p. 153), although the Lord Chancellor has announced a review of the rules on pleading.

Libel has been called a rich man's sport, because the legal costs together with any damages which may be awarded can make libel cases very expensive. Most libel cases are therefore settled out of court in order to hold down those costs.

This is an area of the law which challenges and sometimes confounds even the greatest legal minds. This chapter explains some of the basic principles of libel, so that you can avoid the more obvious pitfalls. As a broadcaster you must be aware of the scope of libel law and know something about the protection the courts have given journalists. Respect the law, but do not let it paralyse you.

What is libel?

A dictionary definition of defamation is that which takes away or destroys someone's good fame or reputation, and there are two categories of defamation: libel and slander.

Libel is the written publication of defamatory matter, while slander is the spoken word. Under the Defamation Act of 1952 the broadcasting of words was deemed to be a publication in permanent form, so broadcasters commit libel even though the words are spoken.

There is such a thing as criminal libel, but cases which fall into that category are extremely rare. Almost all libel cases are civil cases, so this chapter discusses only civil libel.

The law of libel has two purposes: to protect an individual's reputation and to preserve the right of free speech. These two purposes are by definition contradictory, and the law tries to find a fair balance between them.

A radio station is responsible for publishing any libel it broadcasts, no matter who said it or when. The courts do not care whether it was a reporter who uttered the defamatory words or an interviewee, the publisher has to answer for it, and in this case that means the station and you, if you are the reporter, presenter, producer or editor.

If there is an accusation of libel, a judge first has to decide whether the words broadcast were *capable* of being libellous. If the answer to that question is yes, then the case may go to a jury who will decide whether the words *were* defamatory.

Libel has been defined by the courts over the years. It is anything to a person's discredit, or which *could*:

- lower someone in the estimation of others, or
- expose someone to hatred, ridicule or contempt, or
- injure someone's reputation in his or her office, trade or profession, or
- cause someone to be shunned or avoided.

Thus libel falls into two broad categories – people injured in their private reputation, and people injured in their business or professional reputation. It is not unusual for a plaintiff to bring an action alleging breaches in both categories.

Any statement that could lower the *estimation* of someone in the way he or she carries on a business, trade, office, or profession is libellous.

A statement that adversely affects someone's business is not necessarily libellous. Libel concerns people and their reputations. To be libellous, a statement must at least impute discreditable conduct or show that someone is ill suited or insufficiently qualified for that business or profession.

For example, it is libellous to report incorrectly that a doctor has been suspended by the BMA or is a quack. Both reports reflect adversely on the doctor's professional abilities. It is not libellous, however, to report that a doctor has retired from practice when that is not the fact. He may lose a lot of money as a result of the second statement, but it does not suggest that he is not good at his job. He may have a case for some sort of action, but not for libel.

It *is* libellous to report that someone is insolvent or in financial difficulties when that is not the case, even if you have not imputed any blame. People's financial standing is regarded as part of their reputation.

It does not have to be proved that a statement has discredited someone, only that a 'reasonable person' might think it *could* have that effect. This 'reasonable person' features heavily in libel cases, and has changed over the years. The sort of standards which applied in the 1920s do not necessarily apply now, and the reasonable person is what the jury decides is modern and moderate in outlook.

The courts have also said that this reasonable person should be allowed 'a certain amount of loose thinking', i.e. is not necessarily trained to think logically or listen to broadcasts carefully.

A libel action will fail if the statement has lowered someone only in the estimation of a particular group of people. It has to be in the minds of 'right thinking members of society generally'. For example, in a case in Ireland in 1973 (*Berry* v *Irish Times*), an Irish civil servant sued the paper because it published a picture showing a placard alleging he had helped jail convicted Republicans in England. This failed the 'right thinking' test because members of society generally would think it right that those convicted people should be jailed.

The meaning of words is crucial in the law of libel. The reasonable person test is applied to the construction of the words by a judge in considering whether there is a case to answer, and then it is up to the jury to decide the natural and ordinary meaning of those words. Whatever sense or meaning might have been *intended* is irrelevant.

Deciding the meaning of words or phrases will also take into account any inference, implication or innuendo accepted by the 'reasonable' listener. In a case brought against Bristol United Press in 1963, it was held that the phrase 'His name is certainly not George Washington' implies that John Smith is untruthful. It does not matter what witnesses or parties in the case think the words mean, the jury decides what 'reasonable people' *might* understand them to mean.

It also does not matter whether the person hearing the libel does not believe it is true. Even if the statement was broadcast as a joke, and witnesses are called to say they took it as a joke, the jury can still decide that it is libellous.

Juries usually consider the whole of the piece complained of, because there may be 'bane and antidote' – when a piece speaks of a libel in order to disprove it. If you are considering running such a piece, take advice first.

It is not only the meanings of ordinary words that change with the passage of time, slang words change too. In 1858 a judge ruled that the word 'blackleg' had been around long enough for everyone to understand its meaning. He then went on to define it as someone who earns a living by frequenting racecourses and gambling houses, who gets the best odds and gives the least, but does not necessarily cheat others. That definition is still in my dictionary, but would a court today be confident that the reasonable person would use that definition?

Proof

For a libel action to succeed, a plaintiff must prove that:

- the statement is defamatory, and
- it is reasonable for it to be understood to refer to the plaintiff, and
- it was published by the defendant(s).

The plaintiff *does not* have to prove:

- that the statement is false (although if it can be *proved* as *true*, that is a valid defence)
- intent: in many other areas of law, intent must be proved, but in libel the courts will presume intent (except in an 'unintentional' defence – see p. 152).
- that any real damage has been done: it is sufficient that a statement *tends* to discredit the plaintiff.

It is a mistake to think that you can avoid a libel action simply by not naming someone. If the plaintiff can satisfy a jury that the 'reasonable person' would make an identification based on the other material in the report, the case is proved. Not naming someone can create other problems. A local paper once quoted from a report by the district auditor which criticised the deputy housing manager on the local council. They did not name him, but were successfully sued by the new deputy housing manager who had taken over since the time dealt with by the report.

Every repetition of a libel is considered a fresh

publication, so there may be cause for an action every time a libellous tape goes out, or if an apology for libel repeats the libel itself.

Remember that the station is responsible for any libel it puts to air, so it does not matter who first made the offending statement or how important that person is. If the station broadcasts a libellous statement, the station is as liable as the person who said it.

Defences to libel

At this stage, you must be thinking there is really nothing you can put to air without ending up in the High Court (which is where all libel cases are heard). This is where the law tries to strike the balance between protecting people's reputations and maintaining free speech.

There are seven recognised rejoinders to a plaintiff's initial claim of a libel. The first three are repudiations, the best and most final of which is the first one, but if a potential defendant can *prove* any one of the seven, or a combination of them, a libel case may not get past the lawyers' offices.

1. The item was not broadcast by us.
2. The words did not refer to the plaintiff, and could not be understood to do so.
3. The words did not bear, and could not be understood to bear, a defamatory meaning.
4. The words broadcast were authorised by the plaintiff, or consent had been given.
5. The broadcast was privileged.
6. The words were true in substance and fact.
7. The words were fair comment on a matter of public interest.

If a possible libel goes out on air, tell the management as soon as possible and pass the tape on to them to keep in case the libelled person threatens action. Much can be accomplished on the legal side so long as the station is seen to have acted quickly.

Keep conversations with potential plaintiffs short and encourage them to write. Listen carefully to what they say and make notes of the conversation. *Never* admit anything, even if you think they may be right. Tell them that you are not in a position to reply and that if they feel strongly they should write.

Of the seven rejoinders listed above, the last three are defences that are often used in libel trials. Their proper designations are privilege, justification and fair comment, the last two of which are very common defences. We will look at them in more detail below, as well as the defence of unintentional libel, but there are a further five defences of which you should be aware:

1. The plaintiff has died. A dead person cannot be libelled (except in criminal libel), and even if someone has started an action, the case cannot carry on after his or her death.

2. The plaintiff agreed to publication. This corresponds to the fourth rejoinder listed above, and would probably require a signed statement.

3. Proceedings were not started within three years of publication. This is called the statute of limitation. Note it says *started* within three years. (Once a case does get going, it can take as long as a couple of years to get to court.) The statute of limitation was six years until it was changed in 1985, so cases dating back to 1984-85 can still be brought until 1990-91.

4. The matter has already been adjudged. Once the case has been decided, the only way a new case can be brought is if the statement is re-broadcast.

5. Accord and satisfaction. This means that the plaintiff has accepted what has been done as sufficient, e.g. a correction and apology. Never assume you have got accord and satisfaction. Your lawyers will tell you when you have.

Privilege

There are circumstances in which, under the protection of

privilege, the publication of defamatory matter is allowed. Privilege is one of the most important protections offered to journalists. Without it, it would not be possible to report fully on what happens in the courts, Parliament, local councils or most of the bodies which are part of our democratic process.

Under the protection of privilege, any action for libel will fail if the broadcast was a fair and accurate report of:

- Parliament, its committees, or papers (reports, papers, votes and proceedings).
- Judicial proceedings.
- Bodies recognised by law and exercising a quasi-judicial function, e.g. recognised tribunals, commissions, or inquiries set up by government departments.
- The findings or decision of any association formed to promote or safeguard art, science, religion, learning, trade, industry, business, a profession, game, sport or pastime which is empowered by its constitution to control or adjudicate over its members. This covers bodies like the FA, Law Society, BMA, or Jockey Club. Note that privilege covers only the findings or decision, not a report.
- A public meeting lawfully held for a lawful purpose and for the furtherance of discussion of any matter of public concern, whether admission to the meeting is general or restricted (say by buying a ticket).
- Any local authority or committee, and meeting of JPs or Justices acting otherwise than as a court, any tribunal, board, committee or body constituted by or under an Act of Parliament (such as an industrial tribunal or the IBA).
- A general meeting of any public company.
- Any notice or statement issued by a government department, officer of state, local authority or chief of police. (The category does *not* cover leaked documents.)*

*Note that comments made by press officers are not covered by privilege. In a case in 1983, Lord Justice Stephenson said that privilege applied more to statements issued on behalf of a government department than to 'information

Privilege falls into two categories: *absolute* and *qualified*. The first three circumstances in the list are covered by absolute privilege. The rest are covered by qualified privilege and are also subject to explanation or contradiction.

Absolute privilege is enjoyed by, for instance, Members of Parliament who can say whatever they want during proceedings in the House of Commons without fear of action by the Courts. It does not matter whether a statement was true or false, nor whether it was said maliciously. The 1688 Bill of Rights says: 'The freedom of speech and debates or proceedings in Parliament ought not to be impeached or questioned in any Court or place out of Parliament.'

However, the *reporting* of a Parliamentary statement or court proceeding is covered by qualified privilege. In essence, the original speaker may have been motivated by malice, but the reporter must be able to show that malice was *not* a motivation. Your report must also be a 'fair and accurate' account of what took place.

Absolute privilege

The three words *fair, accurate* and *contemporaneous* should be stressed. 'Fair and accurate' does not necessarily mean it has to be a verbatim report. As long as it is fair, you can summarise what went on. Contemporaneous means exactly what it says if you are to claim absolute privilege, e.g. if a libel goes out while Parliament is being broadcast live. In follow-up reports you are covered by qualified privilege.

So far as reporting what happens in the courts is concerned, even though Parliament meant journalists to have only qualified privilege in the Libel Amendment Act 1888, the wording of the Act actually gives us absolute privilege (except in certain sorts of cases or courts, such as

---

pulled out of the mouth of an unwilling officer of the department'. He went on to say that any assumption, inference or speculation by the journalist or press officer would not be privileged.

those involving juveniles). In order to hold on to this, the law specifies that the report must be fair and accurate. The report can therefore be as short as you like provided it gives a summary of both sides, contains no inaccuracies and does not give disproportionate weight to one side. Obviously, during the course of a trial, you cannot present both sides when you are reporting, say, the prosecution's opening speech. But by the end of the trial you should have redressed the balance. You should also underline your uneven approach by telling the listener that the trial is continuing.

Contemporaneous, in newspaper terms, means the first edition possible; in radio terms, it means the first opportunity for the report to be broadcast in a news bulletin or programme. All repetitions of the report are covered by qualified privilege.

If your report contains any inaccuracies, you lose all the protection offered by privilege. If you get a name or address wrong, or summarise the charges wrongly, the law will turn against you rather than help you.

Take care, too, when writing cues for court reports. Do not include anything that could be seen as a misrepresentation or exaggeration, and do not present allegations as though they are proven facts.

Qualified privilege

This defence affords almost as much protection as absolute privilege, so long as the report is fair and accurate. The main difference is that you must not be motivated by malice in your reporting.

Whenever this book refers to malice, it means what the law calls 'express malice', which in legal terms means more than just spite or ill-will. It covers any dishonest or improper motive, knowing a statement was not true, or being 'reckless' with the truth, which means neither considering nor caring about the truth.

Note that unlike absolute privilege, qualified privilege does not have to be contemporaneous, but you must take particular care if you are using information from, say, a cutting of an old court case – privilege does not apply as fully without this third element.

Qualified privilege also offers spokespeople the opportunity for 'explanation or contradiction'. If, for instance, a controversial statement was made by a shareholder during a general meeting of a public company, you would be covered by qualified privilege in reporting it, but someone from the company could insist on an explanation or contradiction being broadcast, if you did not cover it in your report.

Fair comment

Under this defence, the words broadcast must be 'fair comment made without malice on some matter of public interest' and the facts which provoked the comment must be true. 'Public interest' has been held to include:

- The public conduct of anyone who holds or seeks a public office or position of trust.
- Political and State matters (but we are constrained in this by parts of the IBA Act and the RPA: see p. 169).
- Church matters.
- The administration of justice.
- The administration of local affairs by local authorities.
- Books, pictures, works of art, places and species of public entertainment, public performers, actors, singers, dancers. (But not the private conduct of performers. Early in 1989, John Cleese was awarded damages against the *Daily Mirror* for a story they published claiming he was behaving like Basil Fawlty.)
- Anything which may be fairly said to invite comment or challenge public attention. This is a sort of catch-all section which would include, say, comments on the head of a public transport department's decision to double fares overnight.

'Fair comment' does not have to be proved to be true – comment is not capable of being either true or false. But what does have to be shown is that the comment was on established facts in the report and represents an honestly held opinion. The facts must be stated in the piece so the listener has some basis on which to assess whether comment is well-founded. The judge and jury do not have to share those opinions, but they have to be convinced that they are honestly held.

This defence will *not* succeed, however, if there was an imputation of corrupt or dishonourable motives which are not soundly proved. In other words, the law says you can think what you like and publish strong views on matters of public interest, but you cannot suggest someone is 'base or wicked'. The 'comment' has to be one that any person, even if prejudiced or obstinate, could honestly hold. The objective test is whether any 'fair-minded' person could honestly express that opinion on the proved facts.

Comment must also be recognisable as such and not so mixed up with facts or statements that it is difficult for the listener to distinguish fact from comment.

The only time fair comment can succeed if it is based on incorrect 'facts' is if those 'facts' arose in privileged circumstances (e.g. in Parliament or a court).

Justification

Apart from certain exceptions under the Rehabilitation of Offenders Act (see p. 178), it is a total defence to a libel action if a report can be *proved* to be true in substance and in fact.

This defence is far more difficult than it may look because not only do you have to prove the precise truth of each statement broadcast, you also have to prove a reasonable interpretation of the words and any 'innuendo' that might be attached to them. However, in certain circumstances a defence of justification can succeed even if there are some inaccuracies within a report which is otherwise correct. The Defamation Act 1952 says that 'In an action for libel or slander in respect of words containing two or more distinct charges against the plaintiff, defence of justification shall not fail by reason only that the truth of every charge is not proved, if the words not proved to be true do not *materially* injure the plaintiff's reputation, having regard to the truth of the remaining charges' (my italics).

It has also been held that a man cannot claim damages for a character which he did not possess or deserve.

But these are the only real chinks in an otherwise difficult defence. Proving the exact truth of every statement may be possible, but the 'reasonable interpretation' is a minefield. There was a case just after the war, for example, when a local councillor's house appeared to be getting preferential treatment for official renovation work. Even though the local paper checked all the facts very carefully and could later prove them in court, they lost the case because the inference was that the councillor had *secured* preferential treatment.

In a case involving *Construction News* in 1989, the Appeal Court made it absolutely clear that defendants who are relying on a defence of justification should state briefly but clearly their interpretations of the meanings of disputed words before the case comes to court. Lord Justice May said that not doing so made cases too lengthy and costly, often to the plaintiff's detriment. The law says that a defendant is not allowed to use his definition of the words as his defence, but this decision means that the defendant must now disclose what meanings 'he might seek to justify', whether it is the natural meaning or innuendo.

The defence of justification is usually considered dangerous because the court may take a dim view of a persistence in it if it ultimately fails, and the jury may also award larger damages for the same reason. This happened in 1987 when Jeffrey Archer sued the *Star* for publishing an article linking him with a prostitute. He was awarded £500,000 damages after the judge told the jury that the paper had carried on to the bitter end, and if they found in Archer's favour, they should give sufficient damages to 'send a message to the world' that the accusation was false.

Unintentional libel

There is a defence of unintentional libel if you can show that the words were broadcast innocently and without malice, *and* that an offer of amends has been made in accordance with Section 4 of the 1952 Defamation Act.

A live interviewee may make a libellous statement which the station broadcast unintentionally, but the third requirement of this defence means that an offer of amends must have been made 'as soon as practicable' (a case in 1956 decided that seven weeks later was not as soon as practicable – it would need to be more like seven days) and must not have been withdrawn. Amends can be a correction and apology and/or a payment.

To succeed in a defence of unintentional libel, you must prove that:

1. The station did not know of any circumstances in which it could have understood the words to refer to the complainant, or any reason why innocent-sounding words could be defamatory (which could be tricky) *and*

2. All reasonable care was exercised before the broadcast.

The defence of unintentional libel was introduced into the 1952 Act after the *Express* ran a short story about 'Harold Newstead, a 30-year-old Camberwell man' being convicted of bigamy, and was sued successfully by a different Harold Newstead who worked in Camberwell and had not been convicted of bigamy. However, it is debatable whether the *Express* could have satisfied the 'reasonable care' element since their story was so brief that the second Harold Newstead might still have had grounds for suing.

It is also worth considering the famous case of Artemus Jones in 1909. A reporter covering a motor festival in Dieppe invented a character called Artemus Jones in order to give colour to the story he was writing for the *Sunday Chronicle*. The invented Artemus was described as being 'with a lady who is not his wife, who must be, you know – the other thing!' The paper was sued by a real Artemus

Jones, a London barrister, who won substantial damages. A defence of unintentional libel might have succeeded, although the case had complicating factors, among them the fact that the real Artemus was occasionally commissioned to write law reports for the same paper, so it would not have been unreasonable for the reporter to be familiar with his name.

Although circumstances have changed since then, the dangers of inventing characters still exist.

Because of the strict provisions of this defence and the need for a quick response from the station, any unintentional libel needs legal advice – and *fast*!

Precedents to this defence are few, but it is an obvious candidate for settling out of court.

Damages

At the moment, the basic rule juries are given for deciding what amount of damages to award is that they should compensate the plaintiff, not punish the defendant, but the amount should be large enough to allow the plaintiff to be able to show that the 'stain' has been removed.

Exemplary or punitive damages (which means awarding a lot of money) should be awarded only in cases of unconstitutional action by a government official or where it has been shown that the defendant calculated that the advantage to himself would outweigh the compensation he would have to pay.

There is a lot of discussion about how damages are awarded, because juries can be given so little guidance on what is a reasonable amount. In other areas of the law there are guidelines as to what is considered reasonable compensation; in personal injury cases, for instance, judges are given a range of costs within which an award is considered appropriate, depending on the type of injury. This system provides more consistency in the size of awards.

In libel, however, judges are not allowed to give a jury any advice on the scale of damages that might be appropriate. Given that the jury are sitting in judgment for the first time, that means they have no yardstick against which to measure their decision except what they may vaguely remember of previous cases.

The Faulks Committee considered this, and their recommendation was that the judge (who has experience of other libel cases) should decide the level of damages, perhaps with guidance from the jury on the severity of the libel. This recommendation has not been taken up by succeeding governments, and in 1989 Times Newspapers became sufficiently worried by huge awards to make a complaint to the European Commission of Human Rights. They hope to force the government to adopt the Faulks Committee's solution. Times Newspapers' argument is that 'damages have now reached such dimensions that the freedom of an editor to publish what he knows to be in the public interest has been substantially impaired'.

When, later that year, £600,000 damages were awarded against *Private Eye* for a libel concerning Sonia Sutcliffe, the wife of the Yorkshire Ripper, the size of the award provoked widespread adverse comment. Among those who reacted was the Lord Chancellor's Department. A statement said 'The Lord Chancellor is aware of the criticism which is related to many aspects of the law of defamation and particularly the size of libel awards. He is considering proposals for reform which would take all aspects of the law into consideration.'

Private Eye appealed against the size of the damages, but on the day on which the Appeal Court was to assess the case a settlement was agreed out of court. Sonia Sutcliffe received £60,000. Some lawyers thought that all the publicity surrounding this case would mean that juries would award more reasonable amounts.

No such luck. At the end of 1989 a new record of £1.5 million was awarded to the former deputy chairman of the Conservative Party, Lord Aldington, for allegations by Count Nikolai Tolstoy and Nigel Watts that he was responsible for the deaths of thousands of Cossacks and Yugoslavs at the end of the Second World War. The award was for the pamphlet version of the libel; the book version was settled out of court for £30,000. Count Tolstoy has announced plans to appeal against the size of the damages; the appeal was pending as this book went to press.

In the face of mounting criticism, the Lord Chancellor, Lord Mackay, has decided to introduce an amendment into the Courts and Legal Services Bill (which was making its way through Parliament as this book went to press) to enable the Court of Appeal to increase or reduce jury awards. The Court will also be given the power to set benchmarks for other cases, and judges in libel actions will be able to give juries the Appeal Court's guidance when considering the outcome of a case. Even so, Times Newspapers are still waiting to hear whether the Human Rights Commission will accept their case, which would force even more fundamental reforms on the government.

10

Contempt of Court

Contempt is any act likely or calculated to obstruct the due administration of justice, i.e. anything likely to prejudice a fair trial. You can be in contempt of either a criminal court or a civil court.

Contempt of criminal courts

It is useful to think of contempt of court as divided into four bands:

1. After a crime has been committed but before there is a suspect.
2. After there is a suspect.
3. During the course of preliminary proceedings, which will usually be appearances or committal proceedings in a Magistrates Court.
4. During the course of a trial.

What can be reported and how a story can be told changes within each of the bands.

The first band covers the period when, theoretically, you can really run with the story. However, there is a dangerous period between when a crime is committed and when the accused actually appears in court, because you cannot always be absolutely certain where all the pieces fit in. If the police arrest someone at the scene of a crime, or during a car chase, or whatever, the contempt rules apply *from the moment of arrest or warrant of arrest* (see p. 161).

When the police issue an appeal for help in tracing someone for whom a warrant has been issued, it is strictly contempt to broadcast it, but there are no known cases of prosecution, and the Attorney General of the day told Parliament during the debate on the Bill stage of the Contempt Act 1981 at this was a public service and he wanted the media to continue to assist in the apprehension of a wanted man.

But apart from the specific appeal, once a person has been arrested or charged, or a warrant issued, there is no such thing as a 'murder victim', 'robbery victim', or 'rape victim'. There are dead people or injured people, because from now on it is up to a jury to decide whether it was murder, robbery or rape. If you use such words inadvisedly, the court may decide you have affected their judgment and are therefore in contempt.

So at this stage a murder story must run along these lines: 'A man has been charged with the murder of Mrs Ada Bloggs, whose body was found in Smith Square earlier today.' You can say she had head injuries, but not that she was beaten up, or attacked, or battered. Nothing, in fact, which implies a deliberate attack.

The broad rule is that you can report the crime, but you must word your report so that it does not suggest that anyone is the culprit. So you can say *a* man was arrested after a post office robbery, but not *the* man.

You must also never describe someone who has been arrested, because that might prejudice any future defence argument contesting identity. In 1976 Peter Hain was fighting a theft charge, and the *Evening Standard* was fined £1000 because they ran a photograph of him going to an identity parade. The main line of his defence was that it was a case of mistaken identity, and the court held that running his photograph created a serious risk of prejudicing the trial, even though the caption to the photo was 'Hain, he's no bank robber'.

You must be very cautious when someone is 'helping police with their inquiries'. While it is true that the person may be there voluntarily and not charged with any offence, there is no way you can know that. In any case, if someone is there who does not want to be, in law that person has been arrested. If you name someone who is there voluntarily, you are in danger of a libel action later on. Choose your words with care – even skill.

Once the case gets to court, what can and can't be said is strictly specified. During preliminary proceedings, what can be reported is laid down in law (see below), but once the case is being heard in full, reports of what the court hears can start (see p. 163).

The Magistrates Courts Act 1980

Under this Act, every sentence of the following story of a committal contains at least one contempt of court:

> A mother of three from Coolstown has been committed for trial on a shoplifting charge. Blonde housewife, Elsie Jones, was wearing a green trouser suit when she appeared at Peckham Green Magistrates Court. She waved at her children as she left the dock.

You cannot say she is a mother of three, that she is a blonde wearing a trouser suit, or that she waved at her children.

The Act lists the ten points you can report from preliminary hearings for offences triable by jury:

- The identity of the court and the names of the examining justices.
- The names, addresses and occupations of the parties and witnesses and the ages of the defendant(s) and witnesses.
- The offence(s) or a summary of them.
- The names of counsel and solicitors.
- The decision of the court to commit the defendant(s) for trial and any decision of the court on the disposal of the case of any defendant(s) not committed.
- If the defendant is committed, the charges, or a

summary, and the court to which the defendant is committed.

- If the committal proceedings are adjourned, the date and place to which they are adjourned.
- Any arrangements relating to bail, committal or adjournment.
- Whether legal aid was granted to the defendant(s).
- Any decision of the court as to whether these reporting restrictions were lifted.

These restrictions usually apply during appearances in a Magistrates Court when the case might end up being heard by a jury at the Crown Court, but they are in force during any proceedings before the case is heard in full. For example, the law says that people being held in custody before trial must appear before the court every seven days (unless there is agreement from all sides to amend the length of time) while a case is being prepared and before the committal begins. These are colloquially known as 'up and downs', because nothing really happens between the defendant coming up from the cells and being taken back down again. In particularly newsworthy cases a reporter might be sent to the up and down, but the restrictions apply because these appearances are part of the preliminary proceedings.

Reporting restrictions in contempt *do not* apply if:

- A defendant applies to have them lifted. If there is more than one defendant, the magistrates have to decide whether it is in the interests of justice to lift restrictions (unless all the defendants wish them to be lifted).
- The court decides not to commit for trial.
- The court decides to deal with one or more defendants summarily. Even if some defendants are committed, the evidence relating to those tried summarily can be reported regardless of whether it impinges on the case of those sent for trial.
- All the defendants have been tried at the Crown Court. This means that once the main case has finished, you

can report evidence given at committal. It is seldom newsworthy if it was not also used in the Crown Court case, but if it is, it is treated as a contemporaneous report, and therefore privileged.

In the case of serious crimes, some cases have to go to the Crown Court. But in cases where the defendant *chooses* a jury trial, this is often reported even though it is not strictly among the ten permitted points. So far, at least, the courts have not stepped on this practice, because it is seen to be to the defendant's advantage.

These restrictions are heavy and make reporting of some cases very difficult, but they are designed to protect the defendant, a duty the courts take very seriously. So learn what you can report by heart and stay within the boundaries.

Even if reporting restrictions have been lifted, there are dangers of a report being contemptuous. It is obviously contempt to take sides, or imply that anybody is guilty – or innocent – of an offence. And you should never report that someone has previous convictions, even if the police say in open court that they are opposing bail because of them.

Generally, you can be in contempt if a report interferes with the course of justice:

- in a particular case, e.g. prejudicing a fair trial, or
- by obstructing the course of justice generally, or
- by failing to comply with a court order.

The Contempt of Court Act 1981

This Act codified some of the common law on contempt, and was intended to help clarify our position. It applies to both civil and criminal courts.

The Act says that any contemptuous broadcast falls within the 'strict liability' rule. 'Strict' as used here means the courts will presume intent rather than the prosecution having to prove it.

If a contempt case is to succeed the following two elements must be proved:

- that the report creates a *substantial* risk of *serious* impediment or prejudice to particular proceedings, and
- that those proceedings are active.

A substantial risk

As Lord Lane said in defining 'substantial risk of serious prejudice': 'A slight or trivial risk of serious prejudice is not enough, nor is a substantial risk of slight prejudice.'

What the courts actually consider substantial and serious was illustrated when five national newspapers were accused of contempt for the articles they wrote when Michael Fagan was arrested after finding his way to the Queen's bedroom in 1982. Lord Lane decided, against the background of the case, that the *Sun* was not guilty for having said Fagan had a long-standing drink problem. He also decided the *Sunday People*'s report that Palace staff heard Fagan making 'quite absurd and fanciful suggestions' would not have sufficiently influenced a jury to amount to contempt. The article in the *Mail on Sunday*, however, suggested that Fagan had been a guest of the Queen's detective who was homosexual. Lord Lane decided that this had created a mental picture which tended to stay in people's minds and found the paper guilty. It was cleared on appeal, however, by arguing that it was a discussion in good faith of public affairs.

No such luck, though, for the *Daily Star*, which referred to an alleged confession by Fagan to the theft of some wine (one of the charges against him), or for the *Sunday Times*, which exaggerated a charge Fagan was facing and reported inaccurately that a driving charge had been dropped.

Proceedings being active

Proceedings are deemed as being active in *criminal* proceedings:

- When an arrest is made without warrant.
- On the issue of a warrant for arrest.

- On the issue of a summons.
- On an indictment being served, or any document specifying charges.
- On oral charging.
- If an inquest has been opened.
- If it is an appeal, when an application to appeal or an application for leave to appeal is made.

Proceedings are active in *civil* courts when the case is 'set down' in the High Court, i.e. when a case goes onto the waiting list to be heard or a date is set.

In inquests and tribunals proceedings become active when a date for the hearing is fixed.

Proceedings in criminal cases *cease* to be active when:

- The arrested person is released without charge.
- No arrest is made within a year of the issue of a warrant, although warrants can be renewed.
- The case is discontinued.
- The defendant is acquitted *or* sentenced.
- The defendant is found unfit to be tried, unfit to plead, or the court orders the charge to lie on file.

In civil proceedings, a case remains active until it is disposed of, abandoned, or withdrawn.

Tape recordings of proceedings

Tape recordings cannot be made in any court unless the permission of the justice has been given in advance. Even if recording is allowed (which is rare, even though practice directions say judges should accede to such a request; more often tape machines are physically taken away from journalists), no part of the recording can be used on air. If a recording is made, it can only be used to check accuracy. Broadcasting any part of the proceedings is contempt.

It is a subject of debate whether court proceedings should be open to the television cameras, as is the case in many other countries. This is of particular interest to radio, because many of the reservations voiced about television do not apply. The existence of microphones need not intimidate witnesses, and radio cannot accidentally reveal the identity of jurors. As far as editing is concerned, written or voiced reports are already subject to editing, so why should taped extracts be treated any differently?

During the course of a court case

Criminal courts

Once the magistrates or a jury are actually hearing the case, life becomes more tolerable. But the basic rules of contempt still apply. You must not broadcast anything which could be seen to prejudice the trial.

In addition, you must leave out anything that happens when the jury is not in the court room, anything the judge directs the jury to ignore, and anything which indicates a previous conviction unless it is mentioned by the defence, in the court room, while the jury is present. Juries are sometimes sent out of the court room, for instance while submissions are made (such as 'no case to answer') or if there are arguments about the admissibility of evidence. The reason they are taken out of the court room is so that they are not swayed by what is taking place, and you will be in clear contempt of court if you report what happens in their absence. Border Television was found in contempt when it reported the guilty pleas of a defendant in a criminal trial who pleaded guilty to certain charges when the jury were not there, but who then went on to contest others.

The courts also have the power, under Section 4 of the Contempt of Court Act 1981, to order that the reporting of some matters should be delayed. In such cases the eventual report will be considered contemporaneous and therefore privileged when it does come out. But if a Section 4 order is made unfairly you can opt for judicial review under the Criminal Justice Act 1988, if you and/or the station can afford the legal fees.

There are occasions when someone has been found guilty by the jury but there is a delay before the judge passes sentence. This always sparks off debates in the newsroom. Strictly speaking, the Act says restrictions apply until *sentence*, but some judges take the view that it is the jury who need protecting from undue influence, and they are not likely to be swayed by mere media background coverage or reports. Not all judges take that view, however, so unless you know a particular judge's attitude, be sure that a report has been cleared by management before you run it.

When a case ends, a defence lawyer may say that there are plans to appeal against conviction or sentence, but the law of contempt does not apply until the appeal is actually lodged, so there is, in the words of Lord Havers, the Attorney General of the day, a 'free for all' time. Once sentence has been passed, we can run reports or background interviews until the leave to appeal has been submitted, which usually takes days rather than hours.

Civil courts

Most civil cases are heard by judges sitting alone, without juries, and the law worries about the effect media reports might have on juries and lay magistrates much more than on judges. The courts have ruled that judges are trained to consider only the evidence before them and not be unduly influenced by outside events, so any contemptuous statement would need to be particularly severe before proceedings were instigated.

The danger of contempt will be greater, however, if it is a case in which a judge is sitting with lay people, which occurs in some sorts of appeals.

Court of Appeal

Judges sitting in the Court of Appeal (and the House of Lords) are deemed to be above any potential influence by journalists, so contempt would only apply if it fell within the category of 'scandalising the courts' (see p. 167).

Defences to contempt of court

Not knowing proceedings were active

Under Section 3 of the Act, there is a defence in not knowing proceedings were active. To be able to claim this defence, though, you have to prove that you took 'all reasonable care' in establishing that you did not know and had no reason to suspect that proceedings were active. If a story smacks of possible proceedings, you need to check with the police to make sure there is no suspect. To cover yourself, make a note of the time and the name of the police officer or official you spoke to.

Discussion of public affairs

As a result of the *Sunday Times*/Distillers tangle over the drug thalidomide in 1974, Section 5 of the Act was introduced so that a discussion in good faith of public affairs would not be treated as contempt if the risk of prejudice to a particular trial was incidental to the discussion. In other words, if there is a continuing discussion about whether the legislation on Sunday trading laws should be liberalised, the debate does not have to stop because a particular shop is being prosecuted for trading on a Sunday. However, you must not link the particular case with the general discussion.

In 1989 TVS was fined £25,000 for contempt because they broadcast a programme about landlords in the Reading area running sham bed-and-breakfast accommodation and defrauding the DHSS. One of the people featured in the film was also a defendant in a trial in progress in Reading. Although TVS had blacked out his face, he was still recognisable, and the Divisional Court decided that this involved a substantial risk of serious prejudice, and rejected TVS's defence that any prejudice was incidental to the discussion of a matter of general public interest. Lord Justice Lloyd said that the programme dealt with the very subject matter of the indictment charging the defendants,

so he could not accept it as being 'incidental'. If the programme had devoted more time to an attempt to analyse the
cause of this new wave of Rachmanism (tenant exploitation),
it might have escaped the contempt charge; but the court
decided that the dominant feature of the programme had
been to highlight the activities of a small number of landlords in Reading.

Note that neither of the above defences exist if you *intend*
to impede or prejudice justice by your action, or if you are
'reckless' in the sense of not thinking or caring about the
result of your action.

Common law contempt

Most prosecutions these days are brought under the
Contempt of Court Act. The old common law of contempt
was unheard of between 1981, when the Act came into
force, and 1987, when it was resurrected during the
Spycatcher case.

Under common law contempt, there is no test of whether
proceedings are active, only that they are 'pending' or
'imminent', but intent does have to be proved. The law is
vague and makes journalists' jobs difficult, because
reporters and editors have to pre-judge a court's decision on
the imminence of a case. The 1981 Act was, therefore,
greeted with considerable relief. In 1987, however, all the
inherent difficulties reappeared.

Intent

In the *Guardian* and *Observer* appeals in the *Spycatcher*
case, Sir John Donaldson, Master of the Rolls, said that
when there was conduct 'intended to impede or prejudice the
administration of justice ... intent need not be expressly
avowed or admitted, but can be inferred from all the circumstances'. Since 'intent' in law means having regard to the
natural consequences of actions, he was saying that being
reckless with the consequences is equivalent to intent.

Imminence

In 1988 the *Sun* was fined as a result of its campaign to imprison a doctor for the alleged rape of an eight-year-old. No proceedings had begun, but Lord Justice Watkins said proceedings were 'imminent' because a prosecution was virtually certain to be started 'in the near future'. He also said that the editor had become convinced of the doctor's guilt and tried to persuade *Sun* readers to a similar view: 'That is trial by newspaper, a form of activity which strikes directly at a jury's impartiality.'

In deciding that case, the court relied in part on a 1903 case which said it was not so much that the case had begun, more that it had not finished. The 'imminence' of proceedings is vague and uncertain, but the courts will decide on its application depending on all the circumstances of each case.

The *Sun* was fined £75,000 and an application to appeal to the House of Lords was refused.

Even though common law contempt is seldom used now, remember it if you are covering a breaking story. If it is the sort of story that is likely to end up in front of a jury, be mindful of any prejudicial ingredients.

Scandalising the courts

The courts have decided that conduct of judges and decisions of the court are matters of legitimate public concern and debate. However, we must never impute improper motives to anyone involved in the administration of justice, and abuse of a judge or attacks on the integrity or impartiality of a judge or court is prohibited. It is years since anyone has been prosecuted for scandalising the courts. Lord Salmon has said: 'No criticism of a judgment, however vigorous, can amount to contempt of court if it keeps wthin the limits of reasonable courtesy and of good faith.'

*

Do not be cowed by the laws of libel and contempt. As we have seen, the law gives you some protection in both areas. Find a sensible balance between what you know is beyond the pale and self-censorship.

When faced with the red prof button in the studio, always remember the listener. When you push it the listener hears the start of a word, a jingle, and part of a word/sentence. That is not only jarring, but also diverts the attention. Your listener is left wondering what on earth is going on.

You have to make tough decisions fast. That is why you must know at least the basics of the relevant laws. But don't set yourself limits even narrower than those imposed on you – the law already errs on the side of caution.

11

Restrictions on Reporting

Elections and the Representation of the People Act 1983

Election campaigns are full of interest and good copy, but
they are also a source of serious headaches.

Newspapers do not operate under the same restrictions
as the TV and radio during the run-up to elections.
Newspapers can endorse particular party lines, run stories
in accordance with the paper's viewpoint, and carry
election stories and results of their opinion polls on polling
day itself. No such leniency for us.

The Broadcasting Act 1981 and the Representation of the
People Act 1983 (RPA), combine to demand that the
broadcast media show no prejudice or bias. We not only
have to ensure fair and balanced election coverage, we also
have to be able to *show* that we have done so.

Under the Broadcasting Act, we are under a general
requirement to ensure that 'due impartiality is preserved
on the part of the persons providing the programmes as
respects matters of political or industrial controversy or
relating to current public policy'. During the run-up to an
election, that requirement takes on even more weight.

Pending periods

Elections can be divided into four main time bands:

- *Pending before* nominations have closed but after an
  election date has been announced. It is most unwise to

interview or report on the activities of any candidate during this period because it is not possible to identify all the *potential* candidates.

- *Pending after* nominations have closed. All the candidates are known, and discussions and constituency reports can begin.
- *Eve of poll*. No discussion programmes can be aired about election issues, but balanced constituency reports or news wraps can be.
- *Polling day*. No interviews with candidates, no reports *at all* except straight facts about the weather, the rate of turnout, arrangements for counting, expected time of declaration, etc. You are allowed to give factual reports of opinion polls as long as they have not been commissioned by your station.

When the first pending period begins varies according to what sort of election it is.

- *National elections*: from the date at which the intention to dissolve Parliament is announced by the Queen.
- *Parliamentary by-elections*: from the date the writ is issued, usually in Parliament.
- *Local elections*: from 5 weeks before election day.
- *Local by-elections*: from the date of publishing the notice of election.
- *European elections*: from 5 weeks before election day.

The pending period for any election (and therefore the lifting of retrictions) only ends with the close of polls on polling day.

Balanced and equal time allocations

During an election period, we have to present election coverage in one of two ways, depending on what sort of coverage it is. 'Balanced time' in the context of the RPA means a percentage of time allocated to each party, whereas 'equal time' means exactly what it says.

Balanced time applies whenever a candidate is talking about constituency issues, or 'enhancing their standing', i.e. saying why people should vote for a particular candidate. Equal time applies whenever party policy is being discussed.

Balanced time

The amount of time allotted to each party in a local election is a matter of editorial judgment, taking national and local circumstances into account, and the station management will advise you on the percentages. In a national election the balance is determined by the IBA or equivalent national body, and again you will be advised of the percentages. You do not have to make these calculations for yourself, but you must adhere to them carefully.

The percentages will usually be based on the votes cast in the last comparable election and the number of candidates standing for a particular party. A hiccup occurred in the system in the 1979 general election when the SDP was a 'new' party; a special configuration was adopted, based on the number of members they had, their standing in the polls, and so on.

Balanced time not only covers a percentage of time, but the time of day as well. For example, a broadcast featuring one party in the morning drive-time programme cannot be 'balanced' by giving another party their proportion of time in a programme going out at 21.00 because of the difference in the size of the audience. Even within individual programmes, it is good practice to run a series of election reports at about the same time within the programme.

The balanced percentages you are given could look something like this: Conservatives 25%; Labour 25%; SDP 15%; SLD 15%; Greens 10%; all others 10% ('all others' can mount up – it is not unusual for there to be eight or more candidates in a constituency). By polling day, the station must be able to show that it has given each party its correct overall percentage of air time. This is done by keeping election logs (see p. 175).

Some programmes or stations find it easier to restrict their election coverage to balanced wraps so that they know they are always on course. That means that within, say, a 5-minute report each party has the right percentage of air time: in our example, Tories and Labour would each get 1 minute 15 seconds, SDP and SLD would have 45 seconds each, the Greens 30 seconds, and there would be about 30 seconds left for all the others. 'All others' is covered by that bit of the report when you hear the broadcaster saying 'And there are six other candidates running in the constituency. They are ...'. Since those six have only 30 seconds between them, they are each allowed about 5 seconds, so giving their name and party fulfils their time allocation.

If you are putting together a wrap or offering balanced time, all the candidates of parties allocated a percentage must take part or give you written permission to carry on without them. This requirement created real problems during the general elections of the 1970s. The National Front had been apportioned a percentage of time, and therefore had to be included in any constituency report where they had a candidate. The Labour Party made a policy decision not to 'appear on the same platform' as an NF member, which included media coverage. This meant that the broadcast media were confined to compiling constituency reports in only those areas where no one from the NF was standing.

Balanced wraps are a neat way of maintaining balanced time in news programmes or bulletins, but obviously not possible in phone-ins (see p. 174).

Equal time

If you invite parties to send in representative candidates to make policy statements, they must be given *equal* time. It is usually easier to organise equal time contributions as a series of programmes; keeping candidates to equal time within a programme can get very difficult as they all try to pick up on each other's statements. But it is unwise to go ahead with the first programme until you have arranged dates for *all* the participants.

There is an additional problem in deciding which parties to include. The RPA does not necessarily expect you to give equal time to all the 'fringe' parties, but you should consult your management before deciding on a cut-off point.

Candidates

In the period before nominations close, the RPA restrictions apply to any self-declared or provisional candidate or any person who on commonsense grounds *could be regarded* as a potential or likely candidate. That is why it is unwise to interview anyone in the pending period before nominations close. Once the nominations have closed, you have the full list of candidates and therefore know who to include.

Remember, a candidate cannot take part in any programme or report which relates to the election or election issues, or which may 'enhance their general standing' unless either (1) *all* the candidates take part and are given balanced time, or (2) those candidates not taking part give their written consent *and* a balanced report of the activity of those not taking part is included in the programme.

If, say, the three main candidates are each taking part in turn in a programme on successive days, you need the written consent of all the other candidates for each day's programme.

A candidate may also be a party's spokesperson on, say, housing, transport or education, either locally or nationally. As part of your normal news coverage, the spokesperson is allowed to take part *outside* the normal rules of balance. This can only happen when such a spokesperson is dealing with a matter that has total news justification and is not merely enhancing a party's standing. If in doubt, ask your editor or management. However, comments *must* be restricted to broad policy and must not refer to particular matters in a particular constituency. The contributor should be introduced as 'the spokesman on ...' and no mention should be made of his own candidacy or constituency.

Government continues to operate during an election, but the constitutional issues can become very complex. If possible, when you have any doubts, check with your management *before* broadcasting anything. If for some reason that is not possible, presume it is part of the balance, and note it for logging purposes until you can check. Remember that even the Prime Minister is a candidate and should not be allowed to make comments on her constituency or enhance her party's standing.

News not related to the election can be reported. For example if a candidate is in a car accident or has won the pools, that can be reported as long as that person's candidacy is not part of the report. Again, be careful, as some news might be seen to enhance (or undermine) a candidate's reputation.

Phone-ins

A candidate must *never* be allowed on air as a caller, and no candidate or potential candidate should be invited to take part in a phone-in until after nominations have closed.

If a candidate takes part as a guest, then *all* candidates must take part. In a local election, if candidates take part individually on separate days, then each candidate must give written consent for the others to take part on the days when they are not there.

Callers should only be allowed to comment on individual candidates when that candidate is in the studio and able to make an immediate reply.

As with general news or wraps, the time allotted to candidates or parties must be balanced, unless the programme is about policy, in which case the *equal time* rule applies. The complications of getting the balance right mean that it is easier and safer to stick to discussions of policies on phone-ins.

If you have a series of phone-ins on policy matters, the whole of the time the spokesperson for the party is on air is considered to be of benefit to that party. Therefore, if someone from the Labour Party appears on an hour-long phone-in, it does not matter if most of the calls are from anti-Labour people. Since the person is there to answer on behalf of the Party, it is treated as favourable to them and the whole hour is logged as pro-Labour.

General calls put to air must be balanced according to the percentages appropriate for the election or, more probably, comply with equal time if the call is about party policy. That means making a note on the election log which includes the caller's first name, how long they spoke on air and which party benefited. This can be another real headache, for callers sometimes ring to say why they are not going to vote for a particular party without speaking on behalf of any other. In such cases I have been driven to noting 'Sam of Peckham, 3 minutes, anti-Labour' in the hope that other callers will ring to put down the other parties so that in the end they cancel each other out.

News programmes

The same basic rules about the appearance of candidates and balance apply to news bulletins and magazines. Full logs of all election coverage in bulletins should be kept by each newsdesk, unless the bulletin comes from IRN, in which case they will keep track of their coverage balance. Local bulletin coverage must be logged and balanced.

Extracts of speeches by local candidates about local issues cannot be used in either bulletins or programmes unless all the candidates are used according to the balance percentages.

Logs

In order to deal with complaints as well as to be able to show that you have kept within the Broadcasting Act and the RPA, full records must be kept. They must show the name of the programme, date, time and duration of election material broadcast (whether live or recorded), names of participants and the parties represented. In phone-ins, the number of callers favouring each party and the length of time each spoke on air must be noted.

Balanced wraps should be listed as such with their transmission date, time and duration. It is good practice to keep the scripts of all wraps in order to refer back if there are any questions.

Most station managers leave blank logs with each producer or editor so that each programme or news area is responsible for maintaining the correct balance, with the logs finding their way back to management each week or so for a running check to be sure coverage is on course.

The next time polling stations close and an election is over, listen and you will hear the collective sigh of relief from the broadcast media. The kid gloves are back where they belong, and we can get down to covering political issues in the time-honoured way. It may be a compliment of sorts for the law-makers to believe that TV and radio have such a strong influence on the voters, but by the time the polls close, you will be hurling yourself headlong into covering the results and finally talking to one or two candidates without worrying about percentages, balance and fairness.

Rape

The Sexual Offences (Amendment) Act 1976 has been further amended by the Criminal Justice Act 1988 so that a woman's identity is protected from the moment it is *alleged* she has been the victim of a rape offence, and that protection lasts for the whole of her lifetime. Her name can only be broadcast if she gives her written consent. These restrictions apply in any proceedings for rape; attempted rape; aiding, abetting, couselling and procuring rape or attempted rape; incitement to rape; conspiracy to rape; and burglary with intent to rape.

Apart from giving her written permission, the complainant can be named only if:

- The accused satisfies a Crown Court judge before the

trial starts that lifting the restriction is necessary to induce witnesses to come forward *and* his defence will be prejudiced otherwise, *or*

- The judge decides that anonymity puts an unreasonable and serious restriction on reporting the trial and that it should be lifted in the public interest.

Note that you still cannot name the complainant if the man is acquitted!

Until the 1988 Criminal Justice Act came into effect, the accused could not be named unless he was convicted. Now, however, the identity of the accused is no longer protected in law.

The restrictions on naming the rape victim do not apply if rape is merely mentioned in another trial when there are no proceedings going ahead on a rape charge or on any charge other than those listed above, e.g. indecent assault. The name ban can be lifted if the judge consents to a request from an editor or journalist; the request is most often granted, perhaps not surprisingly, in cases in which the defendant faces a charge of murder as well as rape.

Sometimes a patchwork identification can be achieved because some reports give certain details, others different ones. The Press Council has therefore suggested that reporters and editors co-operate with each other and agree about which details should come out.

In 1983 the Solicitor General said that it could be an offence if enough details were given to identify the complainant in the minds of even *some* people, though not to the community generally. Therefore, if your story is about a man who is accused of raping a 60-year-old woman in her flat, you had better be sure that there are enough 60-year-old women living in that block of flats so that no one on the estate will be able to work out her identity.

Children and young persons

The law defines children as being between 10 and 14, and young persons as between 14 and 17. Both are usually dealt with by juvenile courts. Children under 10 are deemed incapable of criminal acts.

The right of reporters to attend juvenile courts is one of the rare occasions when we have a special right which is not afforded to the public at large. However, no report of juvenile proceedings can reveal the name, address, school or any other particulars that would identify any juvenile involved in any way, whether the juvenile is the object of the hearing or a witness. Further, any adult court can prohibit the reporting of any material leading to the identification of juveniles involved in any proceedings before it.

Juvenile courts were established under the Children and Young Persons Act 1933, and their powers have been altered by subsequent Acts, the last being the Children and Young Persons Act 1969, which says that the court or the Home Secretary can lift the ban on identifying a person under the age of 17 *only* in the interests of avoiding injustice to the juvenile.

The law is very serious about protecting children and young people from the gaze and possible censure of the public, so be sure you adhere to the regulations.

Appeals from the juvenile court go to a Crown Court, or High Court, but the restrictions on revealing the identity of the juvenile still apply. A young person can also be sent for trial by jury at a Crown Court if the sentence for the offence is sufficiently serious to be punishable by 14 or more years' imprisonment, such as homicide, robbery or rape.

Juvenile courts deal with more than just crime. They also take action in cases where children (even below the age of 10) are in need of special care. They have the power to take a child from its parents and put it into care, they can order special supervision, or require parents to mend their ways and take better care of a child. In cases of mental illness, they can send children to hospital or appoint special guardians.

Rehabilitation of Offenders Act 1974

This Act was passed to enable someone who has been

convicted of a relatively minor offence to live it down and be protected from having the conviction dragged up from the far distant past. How much time must elapse before a conviction becomes 'spent', and therefore not suitable for reporting, depends on how long a sentence was originally passed.

Any sentence which imprisoned someone for more than 30 months can never be spent. If a person was sentenced for between 6 and 30 months, the conviction is not spent for 10 years, and sentences involving less than 6 months take 7 years before being spent. If no prison sentence was imposed, the rehabilitation period is 5 years, unless the court decided on an absolute discharge, which carries a 6-month period.

Generally speaking, it is not ethical to report spent convictions, but so far there have not been any cases of papers or stations being sued when they have done so in genuine 'public interest'. Court officials, however, can be fined for revealing a spent conviction, and reporters can be jailed for offering bribes to obtain the information.

Breach of copyright

The law of copyright is at least as complex as that of defamation, but most of the pitfalls will be avoided by an agreed payment of royalties or at least the implied agreement of an author who wants publicity knowing that you represent a radio station and that you are recording. But the dangers of infringing copyright remain, and what follows is no more than a very brief guide. If there is any question in your mind, get advice before anything which could be copyrighted goes out on air.

Copyright in broadcast material is held by the IBA or the BBC, and in the case of ILR that copyright is then transferred to an individual station by its licence from the IBA. ILR stations cannot use recordings of BBC broadcasts without the BBC's permission (and usually a credit) and vice versa. If one of the authorities (i.e. the IBA or BBC) has obtained the exclusive right to a programme or event, the other will be in breach of copyright if a broadcast impinges on that exclusivity. For example, for the time being the BBC has an exclusive agreement for broadcasting commentaries from the All England Lawn Tennis Wimbledon fortnight, while ILR is given what is called 'news access'. That means we can report what is happening (as long as it does not exceed 2 minutes per hour), but we cannot offer live, blow-by-blow descriptions of a match.

The Copyright Act 1988, which came into force in the second half of 1989, has replaced the old and much criticised Act of 1956. It is intended make the law clearer and easier to follow; whether it succeeds remains to be seen.

The principle of copyright is to give the 'author' of a piece the right to prevent others reproducing the work without permission. Under the new Act, however, this does not apply to employees of a radio station. The law says that the station is the 'first owner' of staff journalists' material. Freelancers, on the other hand, still hold copyright in their pieces. In principle, therefore, the station needs to get the freelancer's agreement before an item can be passed on for use by some other broadcasting outlet.

The law protects the physical thing, not the idea, so that if, for instance, two authors had the same idea for a plot of a novel, the law would protect how each had written the story, but not the plot itself.

Copyright exists from the moment a work is made and generally continues in existence until 50 years after the work's first publication or the author's death, whichever is the longer.

In the case of broadcasting, copyright remains in force for 50 years from the end of the calendar year in which the author died. Once the author has been dead for fifty years, *all* the works by that author go into the public domain, copyright no longer applies and no royalties need to be paid. Copyright is held indefinitely in an unpublished work. Note that copyright in some works is held by more than one person (the lyricist *and* the composer hold copyright in most songs). In such cases copyright remains in force for 50 years from the death of the longest surviving copyright holder.

There can be no copyright on news, so that even if we broadcast the story first, we cannot claim exclusivity of the facts, only the formulation of the words we used to tell the story. But if another station continually lifts the facts of all the stories we run without making any effort to compile the information for themselves, that might constitute an infringement of copyright.

The law allows us to use extracts from other people's works for the purpose of artistic criticism and review, or for covering news or current events. This falls within the category of *fair dealing*. In deciding how much of the work can be used 'fairly' before there is a breach of copyright, the courts look at the *quality* of what is used rather than the quantity. If in the course of a review only a small portion of the original work is used, but that portion is the vital part, that could be a breach of copyright. The law itself does not give any set figures as to what constitutes fair dealing, but the Society of Authors and the Publishers Association have agreed some practice guidelines. Quotations of up to 400 words, or extracts of up to 800 words (so long as no single extract is more than 300 words), would normally be acceptable. So would reading out fewer than 20 lines of a poem, so long as that was less than 25 per cent of the whole.

In terms of news or current events, it has been held that copyright does not cover the information in a report, but rather the 'literary form in which the information is dressed'. In the compilation of reports, we can quote from documents so long as those documents have been circulated to a wide enough group to make them subject to public criticism. Do not forget that most government documents are HMSO copyright, even though government depart-ments generally encourage wide coverage of their contents.

There have been cases in which even a document marked 'confidential', by being circulated to a progressively wider group of people, has been deemed by the courts to have become well enough known to be open to public criticism. But, as in many other areas of law, each case will be decided on its own merits, so do not take foolhardy decisions on your own.

If the material in question is a commercially published disc or tape, whether it is Michael Jackson or the Goon Show, we have to record the title, author, publisher, disc or tape number, and the duration of what was played on air. It is on the basis of this information that the two main societies of copyright owners assess and collect royalties in order to redistribute the money among those who own the copyright. The societies are the Performing Right Society (PRS) and Phonographic Performance Ltd (PPL), and they also determine each station's 'needle time' (what proportion of air time can be given over to playing records), and how much the royalties should cost for that needle time.

The Home Secretary's ban

On 19 October 1988 the Home Secretary issued a ban on the broadcasting of any words spoken by a representative or supporter of certain organisations. He instigated the ban under his powers in Section 29(3) of the Broadcasting Act 1981, which allows him to notify broadcasters that specified material should not be aired. The ban was incorporated into the Act through emergency legislation in order to, in the government's words, 'starve the terrorist of the oxygen of publicity'. The first paragraph of the notice says that we must:

> refrain from broadcasting any matter which consists of or includes –
> any words spoken, whether in the course of an interview or discussion or otherwise, by a person who appears or is heard on the programme in which the matter is broadcast where –
> (a) the person speaking the words represents or purports to represent an organisation specified in paragraph 2 below, or
> (b) the words support or solicit or invite support for such an organisation,
> other than any matter specified in paragraph 3 below.

The organisations listed in the second paragraph which are subject to the ban are:

Loyalists:
UDF (Ulster Defence Association)
UFF (Ulster Freedom Fighters)
UVF (Ulster Volunteer Force)
Red Hand Commandoes

Republicans:
IRA (Irish Republican Army)
INLA (Irish Nationalist Liberation Army)
Cumann no Mban (The Women's Movement)
Saor Eire
Fianna Na h'Eireann (Youth Movement)
Sinn Fein
Republican Sinn Fein

The ban applies to direct statements and words or lyrics sung or spoken, but not to the reporting of them. That means that we cannot broadcast actuality of anything said by a representative of any of the organisations listed above, but we can *report* what was said, either verbatim or paraphrased. Under paragraph 1(b) of the notice, we also cannot broadcast (but can report) any statement or song which supports any of those organisations.

Even though recordings of court proceedings are not used in this country, if a representative or supporter of a proscribed organisation gives evidence in a court in a country where recording is allowed, then that evidence cannot be directly broadcast in this country. However, a report of the exact words, or a summary of them, could be aired.

Because the notice requires broadcasters to make every endeavour to prevent the words of the proscribed organisations reaching the airwaves, any phone-in or live interview with someone likely to speak in support of them must be in delay.

The notice also covers any archive material of members or supporters of those groups, and even if the old material is a recording of someone who has died, the actuality cannot go out on air.

Exemptions

The Home Office has said that a member or representative of one of the organisations is not necessarily to be considered as permanently representing that organisation, and not all of that person's daily activities should fall within the ban. Therefore, if a member or representative is talking about a situation that has nothing to do with that group (for instance, the circumstances surrounding a car crash), then the provisions of the notice would not apply. However, whether the notice does apply will depend on the nature of the words and the particular context in which they were used (para 1(b)).

The Home Office has also explained that it is not intended that genuine works of fiction should be covered by the restrictions. Therefore, 'a person' as described in paragraph 1 does *not* include an actor playing a part.

The final paragraph of the notice (para 3) also exempts any proceedings or statements made in Parliament, but that applies only to Westminster. Any proceedings or statements in the European Parliament or Parliaments in other countries are *not* exempted.

The other exemption in paragraph 3 is statements by or in support of a candidate in the pending periods for Parliamentary, European Parliamentary or local elections. The first time that applied was in the pending period for the European Elections, during which time, for example, Sinn Fein candidates and their supporters could appear on air, but the ban became effective again on polling day, 15 June 1989. That meant that even if a Sinn Fein candidate had won, no interview with the winner could have been broadcast.

Special care needs to be taken during the course of phone-ins, because a caller purporting to speak on a perfectly acceptable subject may try to switch topics and speak in favour of one of the proscribed groups.

As this book went to press, there was a case making its way through the courts that the Home Secretary had over-stepped his powers, that the ban contravenes the

Convention on Human Rights, and that it prevents journalists from reporting the affairs of Northern Ireland impartially. The plaintiffs, six journalists from different areas of the media who are backed by the National Union of Journalists, think the case may go to the European Court before being finally decided.

Further Reading

Sir Ernest Gowers, *The Complete Plain Words*, Pelican Books. Originally an attempt to get Civil Servants to use ordinary but proper language, it is better not to dip into this book unless you have some time to enjoy the clever barbs it employs in pointing out the misuse of everyday English.

John Silverlight, *Words*, Macmillan. A collection giving the etymology of some words and their modern usage.

Keith Waterhouse, *Waterhouse on Newspaper Style*, Viking. This guide for tabloid papers is largely applicable to writing for any medium.

Robert McLeish, *The Technique of Radio Production*, Focal Press.

Walter Greenwood and Tom Welsh, *McNae's Essential Law for Journalists*, 10th edition, Butterworths. This is widely regarded as the journalist's 'bible' on the law. It is compact and understandable to those of us not legally trained. Remember, though, that it is aimed at print journalists, so the section on election law, for example, does not apply to radio. Although this edition was published at a time when the law was in the midst of many changes, their reading of the eventual outcome is correct.

Geoffrey Robertson and Andrew Nicol, *Media Law*, Sage. Published in 1984, a revised edition from these two lawyers would be most welcome. While certain areas of the law have changed, the principles are still sound.

Sir Brian Neill and Richard Rampton, *Duncan and Neill on Defamation*, Butterworths. A very good guide to defamation without being a massive legal tome.

Index